1

2

Vandamm

Culver

3

Culver

4

Culver

5

6

Van

7

8

9

Richard Tucker, Culver

Richard Tucker, Graphic House

11

Culver

Culver

10

1. RED, HOT AND BLUE
2. ANYTHING GOES
3. ANYTHING GOES
4. GIRL CRAZY
5. ANYTHING GOES
6. TAKE A CHANCE

7. SOMETHING FOR THE BOYS
8. DuBARRY WAS A LADY
9. PANAMA HATTIE
10. ANNIE GET YOUR GUN
11. CALL ME MADAM

Who Could Ask For Anything More

Doubleday & Company, Inc., Garden City, New York, 1955

Who Could Ask for Anything More

by ETHEL MERMAN

as told to PETE MARTIN

To my Mom and Pop who have made all this possible

Who Could Ask For Anything More

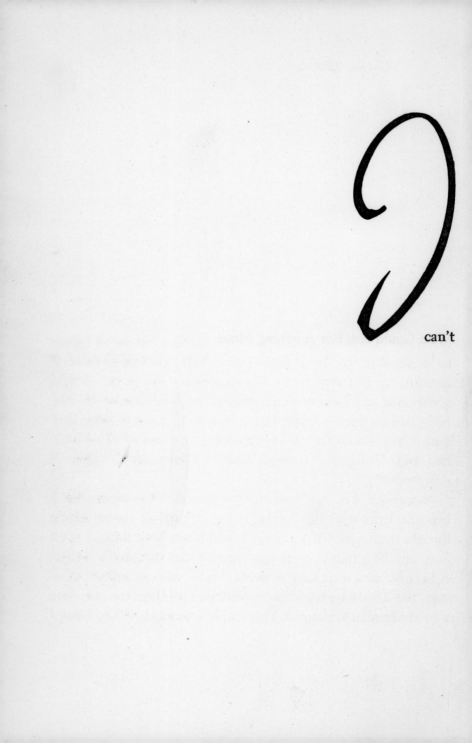

can't

remember ever being afraid of an audience, so I can see no reason to be afraid of you. Even when I was a little kid I never minded standing up in front of people and speaking my piece. I could always sing and I began to entertain when I was five or six. Nobody had to teach me that. I just stood up beside a piano and sang. I didn't think that what I was doing was unusual. If anybody had said, "Imagine you doing that!" I'd have asked, "Doesn't everybody?"

As a singer, I do one basic thing. I project. That means that I belt the lyrics over the footlights like a baseball coach belting fly balls to an outfield. And since I do this one basic thing, I don't have anything that you can analyze and slice thin like a "style." A long list of singers have so much "style" you can imitate them easy, but it's always been hard to imitate me. Have you ever seen a good Merman burlesque? That's what I thought. When I sing I have a whirlwind drive and I don't bother about style, but I do bother about making people understand the lyrics I sing. I honestly don't think there's anyone in the business who can top me at that.

I don't need style to sell my songs; yet, when you hear me, you know who I am. At least I've been told that by a number of honest people and I believe them.

Irving Berlin once said, "If you write lyrics for Ethel, they better be good, for if they're bad everybody's going to hear them anyhow." And Cole Porter said I sound like a band going by. The Peruvian songstress, Yma Sumac, can hit notes that make the dogs come a-running, but her voice is more of a high-frequency vibration job, more like a dog whistle, than a lusty belt from the vocal cords.

When I go to the theater I like to understand what the cast is saying. Fair's fair, so when I sing I make sure that every syllable that comes out of my mouth gets over the footlights in recognizable condition.

One of the things I feel deeply about are those singers who use the melody to vocalize instead of just plain singing and who don't care about the words. Give it a little thought and you'll realize that the really popular singers are the ones who sing the lyrics: Sinatra sings the lyrics, Crosby sings the lyrics, Judy Garland sings the lyrics. Kate Smith and Eddie Fisher sing the lyrics. Nora Bayes sang the lyrics.

Then there're the people who get up and vocalize, which is the word I use for making three syllables out of the word "love" and turning it into "lah-aav-uh." Not long ago I heard a singer in a

Broadway musical—I won't mention his name—whose enunciation was more puzzling than Pinza's in *South Pacific*. When he sang I couldn't understand a word he said. There's an excuse for Pinza's English—he has a genuine foreign accent; but the character I'm talking about is an American. Why can't such people just open their mouths, lay it on the line, and sing the lyrics straight? That's where those expensive lessons come in, with the breathing and the tones, but in the meantime no vowels. I've heard some people sing, particularly sopranos, and if I hadn't been familiar with the lyrics I wouldn't have known what they were singing about. This burns me.

I notice that even some tenors, with high, clear voices, try to sing as if they have marbles in the mouth. Maybe it has to do with proper breathing or head tones, but if somebody asks me, "What language is he singing in?" I answer, "Concert English."

My voice is always getting me in trouble when I'm trying to talk quietly. If I tell a secret, the people in the next room can hear it and understand it. Once I was out to dinner and the headwaiter kept suggesting that we try the roast beef. When I thought he was out of earshot, I said, "Sounds like the house is pushing the beef." He was all the way across the room, but he heard me.

He came over and said, "It is *very good* roast beef."

He was right. The beef was much better than the entree I ordered.

If a song is a hit, I'll do right by it. If it's just an average song, I'll give a little something extra to help make up for what it lacks. If a line is a wow of a line, I'll get the wow out of it, and if it's only so-so, I'll find some way of twisting it or giving it a deadpan reading that it still will get a laugh.

When I work I work harder than anybody and when I play I play harder than most. When I go to a party I've got my little anecdotes and jokes, or I sing easy and I mix easy. I can go out with a policeman or the Duke and Duchess of Windsor and have an equally good time.

The way I feel about my work brought this statement from Ed Sullivan right after Sam Snead's famous missed putt that cost him a championship. Ed said, "I imagine that, to Ethel, Sam Snead's misputt was one of the seven wonders of the world. 'How could he miss it?' she'd reason. 'He plays golf all the time, doesn't he? And he was using his own putter and no one was throwing rocks at him.'"

These remarks of Ed's were based on my philosophy; if you learn your songs and your lines and your stage business, how can you miss? I figured that Sam Snead should know what he was doing too. After all, it was his life's work!

Buck Crouse and Howard Lindsay, the authors of *Call Me Madam*, wrote this line for the program of that show: "The character played by Miss Merman has no resemblance to anybody, living or dead." I thought it an amusing take-off on the usual guff about how any resemblance to a real person is purely coincidental. I'm not a girl who has to move her lips to get the meaning of a headline in a tabloid. On the other hand I'm not a bookworm either, but I do know this much: the character you put down on paper for an audience to read (instead of listen to it) had better bear more than a coincidental resemblance to real life.

12

The way I see it, if you're telling the story of your life, making people understand your lyrics is the big thing. So it figures that if I make this loud, brassy, and honest, the way I did when I sang "I Got Rhythm," "Eadie Was a Lady," and "I Get a Kick Out of You," it ought to go over.

I'm not worried about the honest part. That's no trick. My former husband, Bob Levitt, can vouch for that. Once, when somebody was trying to think of a title for a movie I was to be in, Levitt said, "No problem. *Tactless Tillie Strikes Again*."

During World War II, Levitt was an aide to a general I'll call General W., because his last name doesn't start with that initial. One Sunday afternoon I was dragged to an Army cocktail hoedown with Levitt. General W. had told my husband to bring me. "You've never had your wife to any of these things, Levitt," he said, huffing and puffing. "Why not, Levitt?"

It is an aide's job to follow his Old Man around and make sure that he doesn't trip over his shoelaces or lose his shoulder stars or something. The party was so military that I mentally stood at attention all the time, and I found myself up to my eyeballs in Army wives. Levitt had departed for other parts of the room and I was on my own with all these characters. There were about a hundred people clanking around, and they couldn't have been less my kind. I didn't know anybody, and what with all the yaketying, I didn't find out which of the fifty dames there was Mrs. General W.

The drinks they were serving were warm manhattans, and while I'd never had a manhattan in my life—in fact, I hate them—I thought if I sloshed enough of them down they might dull my senses. There was no choice—either warm manhattans or smiling and showing my teeth.

After the cocktail party we all went over to the Officers' Club to tie on the feed bag. During dinner the band played, and a lady came up to me and said, "Would you mind getting up and singing a few songs?"

I looked at her, wondering, *Who put you in charge, honey?*

I said, "Get out of my way, Cuddles, or I'll spit in your eye."

Levitt told me later, "You said it as if you meant it!" I gave him a clue. I *did* mean it.

Guess who she was? You've got it right away—the general's wife. If they'd had K.P. for officers, Levitt would have drawn ten years' onion peeling. Anyhoo, there was no more urging me to sing. The general's wife turned out to be a nice little woman who thought me funny. She smiled at the other ladies, and her smile said, "Aren't show people quaint?" They all smiled dutifully back at her because she was the general's wife.

My trouble was that Broadway and the Army didn't mix. Army wives have to know protocol and when to be nice to the general's *Frau*—that kind of junk. Also a lot of the people you ran into at those service shindigs were squares. Levitt (the dog) used to tell me that he'd made arrangements for me to pour at the Officers' Club teas. I was petrified until he let me up off the floor.

Quite a sense of humor, that Levitt had. He could mix with any group, it was all the same to him, but when I had to listen to that Army-wife lingo I goofed. They talked about where they'd been stationed and what they did when they were stationed there. Not for me, sister!

14

So whenever anything happened that gave little Ethel a chance to louse up protocol and Levitt's chances for a step up in rank at one and the same time, I was home free. The following horror story of Ethel Levitt as daddy's helper will show that. It took place when we were playing rummy. The general insisted upon playing rummy—not gin, but the old-fashioned kind where you pick up the whole deck and hold about three hundred cards in your hand.

"This is the only kind of rummy I play," he told us. "I never lose at this game," he added grimly. "Never. I'm very fortunate."

Levitt gave me a long, slow warning glare to make sure that I got it and would do the diplomatic thing. But somehow I missed locking looks with him and I didn't get the word. I murdered the general at his own Stone Age caper. I took every round from him. He was so mad he got up and stamped around until I felt like saying, "Stop with the road work, General!" then he stamped out, mumbling something about how he wasn't "going to play with any female cutthroat."

Levitt swore he said "hellcat" instead of "cutthroat." Anyhow, it was a good thing the general chickened when he did. I was afraid he'd have a stroke, so I was happy when he blew.

But while I may have been the dope of the world at the old Army game, I did all right at entertaining the boys at the camps. I liked to go to the staging areas most of all. Those were the most important, because sometimes, after you'd gone there and entertained the boys, they'd march out of the hall onto the bull train, headed for the war, and that was the last entertainment

15

they had. Not to patty-cake around with it, it was the last enter-tainment some of them ever had.

I concentrated on them and I kept concentrating after I be-came pregnant with baby Bob, who was born in 1945. The maternity dresses the girls wore then had elastic around the waist. As you got bigger, it stretched. I haven't worn one since, so I'm not hep to what they're doing these days. I understand they have big round holes cut out in the front of the skirts they wear under smocks, and you have to be careful not to put your knees through them.

The Army stage hands and electricians got a kick out of light-ing me. They knew that I was from the theater and that I knew good lighting when it hit me in the face. So they lit me beauti-fully, with a special sort of off-pink spot. But, as I grew bigger and bigger, the spotlight got smaller and smaller. When I was at Camp Shanks, a month before the baby was born, they had a spot just on my face. I was blacked out from the chin down.

I will say this: whether honesty is the best policy or not, I'm more honest about myself than some of those who've written about me. Every celebrity gets slugged over the head with stuff somebody has dreamed up to pad out a story about him or her. I've seen it in print a couple of times that I was once so naïve that I applied for a passport to get to New York from Astoria. I've never been *that* dumb, even when I was young.

They used to kid me about Astoria—I didn't move to New York until 1933, when I shifted there with my parents—and about how I lived "in another country." I may have said, "O.K., I'll get

16

a passport so I can get to New York." If I did, naturally I didn't mean it. It was for laughs.

And I've been quoted as saying about Mary Martin: "She's all right if you like talent." It's a great crack. I wish I *had* said that one.

Then there was the time when I was in *Annie Get Your Gun* that a New York columnist started the darling little rumor that I was pregnant. It could have ruined the show. If we hadn't had a million-dollar advance sale when this was printed, it could have shuttered us and a lot of people would have been out of work. The rumor became the plague of my life. My obstetrician was even calling me to check, until I told him, "Don't call me. I'll call you." Even after the rumor had been corrected—but not by the columnist who started it—people kept calling the box office to say, "I have tickets for such and such a date." They'd name a date three or four months away and ask, "Do you suppose Miss Merman will still be in the show then? I've waited so long to see it, I'd hate to turn my tickets in now."

The report that I was expecting a child kept popping up at intervals for thirty months. If it had been true, it would have been the oldest baby ever born. I'm not the self-conscious type, but it began to get me down, to have people everywhere I went look at my mid-section before they looked at my face.

When I asked the columnist, "Where did you get your information?" I was told, "Someone in your cast told me." Until then, I'd wondered why it hadn't been checked with me; but after that I stopped wondering. Of course, *anyone* in the cast would know more about such a matter than I.

Chapter Two

Bob Levitt would have told this columnist the truth if he'd been asked. He was always honest about such things. I got a boot out of a remark of his I read: "I like Ethel best of all when she's pregnant."

It was a wonderful crack. When you first heard it you wondered what he meant. It could have meant anything, but what he really meant was that when I was expecting I was sweet and cheerful, and nothing bothered me. Looking forward to a baby coming made me that way. And another thing, we stayed home and we didn't go out as much then, because when I got pregnant I didn't fool around about it. I never had a sick day and my two children were Caesarean births; so I wouldn't call either Little Bobby or Little Ethel a hard, tough pregnancy, but with both children I grew enormous in a big way. Along about the third month, I felt that I was pregnant all over.

Although I'm not married to Levitt any longer—I'll go into the reasons why I'm not later—we certainly started out on a note of honesty. Not diplomacy, just honesty. The two aren't necessarily the same.

I met Levitt through friends at Dinty Moore's after going to a theater. Those friends were Walter Young, then an executive of the New York *Journal-American*, and his wife Ella. Levitt was with them. I had never set eyes on him before. For that matter, he'd never seen me before either, even on the stage. He never went to musical comedies. He didn't like them.

After dinner we went to a night club, but I had to go home early because I had a matinee the next day. Although Levitt hadn't talked to me much during the evening, Walter asked him to take me home. Levitt broke down and talked a little on the way but it was not what I'd call inspiring. There was a snowstorm, but we'd managed to grab a taxicab, and when we pulled up in front of 25 Central Park West, where I lived, the snow was piled high on the curb. Naturally I expected my escort to get out and help me to the sidewalk, but he made no move to get out of the cab.

"Well?" I said.

"This isn't love," he said; "this is just friendship."

"If I never see you again, it will be too soon," I remarked, to give a ladylike translation to what I really told him.

So I got out and plowed through the snow by myself. It was a little different from the Sir Walter Raleigh and Queen Elizabeth overcoat-across-the-puddle thing. For all Levitt cared, I could have got out on my hands and knees.

Even before that, he had indicated that he wasn't the soft, yielding type. I'd asked him for a piece of chewing gum, but he'd made no move to buy me a pack.

The day after this big snow scene he sent me a whole carton of gum. Then, two or three nights later, the Youngs called me again. They were at Toots Shor's, Levitt was with them, and they wanted me to join them. It was my turn to play hard to get. "Nothing doing, that's all," I said. Levitt wasn't going to win me over with any stale old carton of chewing gum. However, he kept trying, and finally we stepped out formal to El Morocco, both of us gussied up in evening clothes. After that, I saw a lot of him.

At that, I prefer the Levitt approach to being drenched with buckets of sweetness and light. I never know where I'm at with people who are too gracious. One St. Patrick's night I was on a double date with Eleanor Holm—I remember we wore green carnations in our hair—when Lady Sylvia Ashley came along and gave me a big, gooey hello, although I've since figured that she was sure she was being gracious and courteous.

"Oh, Miss Merman," she said, "I've never had the pleasure of meeting you, but you're a great, great artist. You're simply delightful."

I don't go for that la-de-dah stuff. I don't care a hoot whether you tell me I stink or tell me I'm good, as long as I'm sure you're leveling with me. When I'm in any doubt at all, my policy is mow 'em down. So I looked her straight in the face and said, "Thank you, Mary Pickford."

To give him his due, Levitt has a sense of humor mixed with

forthrightness. Which brings me to a story I want to work in here about the Duchess of Windsor—and steak tartare, which is the Social Register name for a raw hamburger. We'd been at a party somewhere, but we'd left early. It was when the Duke was writing his book, so he was home writing it, and there were Russell Nype, the Duchess, some other man whose name I forget, and I. Being taken suddenly hungry, we dropped into the Cub Room at the Stork Club, and I ordered a steak tartare sandwich. I love them. I eat them by the pound. I don't like them all sissied up with the anchovies and the stuff they load on if you don't tell them not to. Just give me the raw meat.

"Girl, what did you order?" the Duchess asked me. She always calls me "girl."

"Raw meat," I said.

"Bring a large order, waiter," she said. "I've never had any. I'm terribly curious."

So a whole big thing of raw meat was lugged in. She wolfed it down and thought it wonderful. I guess it's not important, but it seemed so incongruous. I mean, after all, this is a woman who inspired a king to give up his throne because of her loveliness. Well, a raw meat sandwich is not exactly the kind of thing you'd think she'd go for, is it?

Anyhow, mentioning the Duchess leads into Levitt's crack about the Duke's humming. When you're talking to him, the Duke keeps going, "H'm'm'm," between remarks. Maybe it's a nervous tic of the voice or something. I wouldn't know. But he does hum.

I remember asking Levitt, "What's with that noise that comes

21

out of the Duke while you're talking to him? Why do you suppose he does it?"

Levitt gave it some thought. "Well," he said seriously, "maybe the Waldorf is DC and the Duke is AC."

I thought it was a very funny remark. If you've ever tried to plug an alternating-current electrical cord into a direct-current outlet, you'll know what he meant. If you haven't, skip it.

For a while after that, when the Duke came up to me, I'd break up and laugh and have to walk away from him.

Speaking of diplomacy, there are certain types who're always getting up impromptu competitions to prove they know more lyrics of bygone pop songs than anybody else. More and more people seem to be doing this nowadays, particularly with old songs being revived all the time, such as Les Paul's and Mary Ford's rendition of "In the Good Old Summertime."

It so happens that I know a number of old lyrics too. I've made it my business to, so when I go to parties and someone sits down and plays them I can sing. And I sing them in spite of the jerks who look at me like I'm Dame Sybil Thorndike, or a lady spy in the Civil War, or something equally mossy, and say, "So you remember *those* lyrics?"

One night when a "gentleman"—I won't mention the name—gave me that "Imagine you recalling *those* old words" routine, I said, "Listen, Galahad! I know the lyrics to 'The Star-Spangled Banner,' too, but it so happens that I wasn't around when they were written."

Speaking of "The Star-Spangled Banner," every year the Joe Cottens give a Fourth of July party. As you come in, you're given a little American flag. The girls stick them on their dresses or in their hair. There's a big brass band a-rooting and a-tooting and the Cottens serve a wonderful luncheon in a big tent. First the band plays down by the pool. Then at twelve-fifteen mint juleps are served. About two or two-fifteen a buffet luncheon is gotten up and the band moves to the tent. Last time I was there, Lenore —that's Joe Cotten's wife—asked me to do a little something patriotic, with the band, like singing the "Banner." So I got up and put my lungs into it.

It so happened that there were a lot of large American flags overhead. There was no breeze—it was a warm day—but as I sang the lyric about the flag still being there, a breeze came out of no-where and the flags unfolded and began to move. It made me feel funny. It was kind of spooky.

Cole Porter was there. And he came over to me and said, "I always knew you had an unusual voice but I didn't know it could reach up and unfurl flags."

The "Banner" is supposed to be hard to sing. It has a terrific range; it goes way up, according to what key you sing it in, but there's a girl, Lucy Monroe, who's made a reputation singing it. I don't know how I happened to take the play away from Lucy this day I'm about to describe, but they gave Joe DiMaggio a Day at Yankee Stadium and they asked me to sing the anthem. I stood on home plate with an accordion player, and bounced that song off the left-field wall the way Joe bounced baseballs from the same spot.

I'd sing, "Oh, say can you see . . ." and about a second later, "Oh, say can you see . . ." would come back to me.

I was married to Bob Levitt at the time, and my pal Peter Lind Hayes nicknamed me Lucy Levitt after Lucy Monroe. From then on, Peter and his wife Mary Healy have always given me that Lucy tag when they see me.

Some of the samples I've given of Merman-type honesty may seem to make a bum out of the old saying, "Honesty is the best policy." But come hot or cold, hard or soft, sweet or sour, some of us can't play it any other way. Leonard Lyons' wife Sylvia is like that. Leonard has a theory that all of his friends ought to be friends. With this in mind, he arranged a party for Perle Mesta and me to meet each other.

As Leonard tells it, what happened next was this: "Mrs. Mesta telephoned from Washington and submitted a list of four dates when she'd be free for dinner. My wife, believing that no dinner table can be considered enviable unless it is graced by the presence of Joe DiMaggio, startled the famed Washington hostess by telling her, 'Before I pick the date I must consult the home-games schedule of the New York Yankees.' "

A few days after that party I came home one afternoon and a maid who was working for me at the time said, "Some crackpot called this afternoon and said she was Margaret Truman."

"It probably was," I said. "I met her the other night at the Lyonses'. What made you think she was a crackpot?"

"I thought she was one of your fans," she said.

I'm still trying to figure that one. She didn't mean what I thought she meant, did she?

Arthur Schwartz once told me a wonderful story about Jimmy Durante and the billing for *Stars in Your Eyes*, that put my darling Schnozz right up there along with Sir Anthony Eden or any old Southern colonel you name in the tact-and-diplomacy dodge. Dwight Deere Wiman was the producer, and naturally it was Wiman who talked to Jimmy about money, but when it came to the question of whether Jimmy would take second billing or co-starring billing, Arthur said he called Jimmy and Lou Clayton, Jimmy's manager, in California himself.

"Jimmy's got to have first billing," Clayton said.

Arthur appealed to Jimmy's gallantry and chivalry. "Jimmy," he said, "you remember the one-act plays Noel Coward wrote for Gertrude Lawrence and himself? Noel was not only the author of the play, he was the star; yet he allowed Gertie's name to go ahead of his."

Arthur says there was a moment of silence. Then Jimmy got it and came through like the natural-born gentleman he is. "I see whatcha mean," he said. "She being a girl and all that." That Jimmy is a doll. I can just picture him saying it.

One newspaper lad who looked me over carefully, then rushed to his typewriter to describe me physically, thought he was being a diplomat too. Maybe he was. He wrote, "Her conformation [meaning mine] is refreshingly different from the standard assembly of a moist mouth, an inflated bosom, two interminable thighs, and a vacant stare."

I didn't know who this guy was who looked over my points or I would have asked him what's so wrong with an inflated bosom, two interminable thighs, a moist mouth, and a vacant stare? I've got news for him. A studio whose name rhymes with box has found that kind of equipment meat and potatoes, and has parlayed it into the most written-of and talked-about chassis since Henry Ford's flivver. Hi there, Marilyn!

But since this expert has brought it up, and since I'm making a point of being honest about myself in this story, maybe it's an idea for me to stand off, take a look at myself, and describe myself physically, giving the good with the bad. Whether it will be the same description my stage and screen audiences would give me, I wouldn't know.

Take my teeth. They're crowded, especially the lower ones. But the top teeth are straight, and they're all mine.

Take my hair. They kid me about my hair and the funny topknot I wear piled on my head. People say, "Get that pompon on her, willya? Boy, is it a freak!" O.K., so it's no gamine do (which is French for idiot boy's hairdo or Frankenstein, Junior Miss Class, hairdo) but it's done all right by me so far, so I'm keeping it.

I talked it over with Walter Lang, the director of my last movie, *There's No Business Like Show Business*. I wanted a new style with maybe a soft wave, but Walter wouldn't go for it. "No, no, no," he said. "People know you this way. It's your trade mark. Don't change it."

Walter is very smart.

I've been told that it must make it uncomfortable for me to wear hats. The answer is, I don't wear hats. The last hat I had was Easter before last. I went into a Fifth Avenue chapeau salon and had an Easter bonnet made, especially for my kind of hairdo. I said, "I want a hat made to accommodate my horse's tail" (I had one then, in addition to the topknot). So the custom-made department of the joint made me a bonnet. It looked like a Salvation Army doll's headpiece. In the back, they cut a hole for the curls to go through. It cost me seventy-five clams, and I wore it only twice. After that I decided that a little old veil worn over my head would do very nicely for Sunday worship, thank you.

In *Annie* I was supposed to wear the kind of old slouch felt hat that the pictures of Annie Oakley always showed her wearing. But I wouldn't wear it, and I wouldn't change my hair from the first minute of the play to the last. I wore it long in back and up in a pompadour in front. Mary Martin, who played the role, wore it up and she wore it down. She wore hats and she wore it in braids. She wore it any old way the whim of the moment hit her. She didn't care. Only I've noticed a very interesting thing. Since Mary cut her hair like a boy's for *South Pacific*, it's been cut the same way ever since, only for *Peter Pan*, even shorter.

There've been about fifty gals who've played the part of Annie and they all changed their hairdos as Annie got more education. As she became more of a lady the hair became more refined. Me, I wouldn't do anything or wear anything on my head during the run of that show that would destroy my hairdo. It took too long to comb it in the first place. I couldn't have made the changes I had to make if I had to comb my hair every time.

It takes longer to do my hair, to comb it out the way I want it. I don't think it's a mental fixation with me. Well, maybe it *is* kind of a small fetish at that.

I put what Cole Porter says about my hair under the heading of Diplomacy. Being very international-set, Cole says my hair makes me look like a modern French painting by Manet or

Renoir, or whoever. That's the first time my topknot has been compared with art. It's been compared with everything else, even a pooch's hairdo. My daughter Ethel says, "Midnight's got the same pompon cut you've got, Mommy." Midnight's the French poodle member of our family.

Speaking of Manet and Renoir, I have a Renoir, a Monet, and a Dufy on my walls now. From hacking around to different galleries I've picked up a little thissa and a little thatta, until I'm as knowing as the average Judy about such matters. I wasn't in the beginning. One story—of the many that Howard Lindsay and Buck Crouse like to tell about me—goes back to the time when I knew from nothing about art. Howard and Buck seem to think it amusing. It goes this way: I'd just had my apartment re-furnished. I'd had some nice things put into it, including some furniture, and in telling them about it I said, "And over the fire-place I've got an original."

"An original what?" Howard and Buck asked eagerly.

"An original, you dopes," I said. "Just an original. That's all."

I found out later that the chic thing to do would have been to give them the name of the artist, but I didn't think that impor-tant. The man at the gallery who'd sold it to me had just called it "an original"—"Now here's an original you ought to have" and "This is an interesting original"—so that's what I called it.

I'm not that simple now. I only enjoy paintings if they're rest-ful to the eye—not anyone else's eye—my eye. Phooey on this fellow Braque, who does paintings of men looking like consump-tive bums. I don't go for him. I'd go to Eleanor Holm's and Billy Rose's place when she was married to him, and every time

I went over there and looked at Billy's Picassos they drove me out of my mind. Some of them were the most gruesome-looking things I've ever seen. Billy had put out fifteen grand for one of them—a still life of some fruit. When I heard that, I said to Eleanor, "Fifteen thousand bucks! I could buy all of that fruit for thirty-five cents, and eat it besides."

But to continue with the physical rundown. Take my legs. This puts me on a spot, because, to be real honest about it, most people—including myself—think I have nice gams, although maybe I shouldn't say it. And there've been no complaints about me in the Jane Russell department either. Period.

I don't have bad arms, and lots of folks think I have expressive hands. And I have small ears, that lie flat against my head. As for my eyes, I've been told that I'm round-eyed and look surprised. What's wrong with that? I think "surprised" is a good way for a dame to look—although it went out with the waltz. Who wants a girl who knows everything?

Let's put it this way: "I use my eyes the best way I can to get the most out of them, particularly when I'm on a sound stage or just an ordinary stage, standing in a spotlight. At such a time, having my lashes spiked with cosmetics helps. Sometimes I don't have to say a word to get my thoughts across to an audience: I just give them a look and my eyes tell the story.

As for my bad points, I wish I had a thinner nose. When I say that, people tell me, "Don't be silly. Your nose is O.K. It goes with your face, doesn't it?"

I don't know about that, but if I could be all made over again,

I'd like a different-shaped face with my different nose. Make mine a face with high cheekbones, like Marlene Dietrich's, please.

Another of my bad points has been taken care of now. I used to wear clothes that were too fancy. One of my best pals, the playwright and writer of lyrics, Dorothy Fields, said of me not long ago, "Merm has chic now. She understands simplicity and the value of clean lines, but I can remember when there wasn't room on her for all of the frills, furbelows, furs, and jewelry she wanted to wear. Anything Mermsy couldn't wear she carried over her arm."

Well, I've learned. Now, when you see me on the street, it's practically impossible to tell me from any other woman. I once felt the same about stage make-up. The more the better, I thought. I was the girl who went all out for everything.

As for other personal weaknesses, I read the Hollywood *Reporter* and the daily and weekly *Variety,* to find out what's what. And I usually go through Winchell and Lyons and Sobol, but that about wraps it up. I tried reading books, but the only time I had for it was when I got home from the theater at night. And even if I came straight home from a performance, I didn't get home until midnight or a quarter past twelve. And I'd be so tired that I'd raid the icebox, stack myself a sandwich and guzzle a glass of milk, then go upstairs and conk off.

I tried to start a book a few times, but after the first three or four pages I dozed off. I was in such a smog that the next night I'd have forgotten those pages I had read and I'd have to start all over again. I never got beyond those three or four pages so I gave it up. I thought, *This is not for me and the hell with it.*

As for daytime reading, the days are always so cluttered I never have time to sit down for an hour of reading.

In spite of having more of what a friend of mine named Eadie used to call "savoir-fairy" than most people, Cole Porter can be honest too. Cole and a buddy of his have a game they play that involves Irving Berlin. When they see Irving coming they look at their wrist watches and make a five-dollar bet. Then they pick a topic and start in on it. Anything will do: Victor Moore, Mount Everest, volcanoes, Eskimo Pies, Philadelphia, the Dalai Lama of Tibet. The bet is based on the number of minutes it will take Irving to bring the conversation around to one of his own songs, no matter where it starts. The average time is said to be less than five minutes.

I wouldn't go so far as to call this ego on Irving's part. It's just that he's so absorbed in his work and so intense about it that what he writes is the most important thing in the world to him. This is no knock to Irving. To me, he doesn't seem so much egotistical as enthusiastic. Every time I see him I like that little man better. We get alone fine.

Speaking of being absorbed in your work, Cole once told a writer who was trying to interview him, "If I don't seem to be listening to what you're saying, it's because I'm writing a song in the back of my head." Sometimes he's so absorbed, he's in another world. As Cole put it, "Some people think work is a four-letter word. I don't."

While I'm at it, there's another kind of honesty. A dame named Ann Pinchot once wrote that the thing that she liked most about me was my honesty in appreciating my own success. "No false modesty for her," Pinchot wrote. "She's glad to be on top, and she admits it."

I wouldn't say she scored a clean miss. I'm grateful for the things that have happened to me, but I'm willing to face the fact that I've done all right, too, instead of giving out with that phony, "It really wasn't anything, fellas," line.

They say it's a good idea to inject a little struggle into the proceedings when you're telling the story of your life, but there was no period when I had to worry where my food was coming from. Pop always kept us in comfort. Mom and Pop are two of the happiest people I've ever known. Our family life is warm and friendly. I adore them and they adore me. In my teens, when I was a secretary, I was happy to be a secretary. So where's the struggle?

While I was a secretary, I sang a little and tried out in a few clubs, but the business of hoping someone would hear me and give me a break didn't last long. I was ambitious enough during this period, but it was no rags-to-riches routine or even gags-to-riches, as it was in the case of some of the comedians I know who own solid platinum Cadillacs.

So my story will be a switch on almost every theatrical story ever told to date. All of them have to do with wearing out shoe leather on sidewalks, and sitting for hours in offices waiting for this producer or that producer to say, "I'm not casting just now, sister." I didn't wear out a single shoe.

One day last summer when we were shooting the picture, *There's No Business Like Show Business,* Johnnie Ray said that he *knew* he was going to be a star when he was five years old.

When Johnnie said this, we all collapsed in wild laughter but I don't know why it should have fractured me. Even when I was a tot I hoped to go on the stage someday and amount to something. I had a voice, and if a voice is there, it's there; all it needs is an opportunity to be heard. I suppose that there's a chance you might never have that opportunity. I think I would have made one anyhow. Somehow or other, I would have come forth, or even fifth, to coin a corny crack.

The way it worked out, I made Cinderella look like a sob story. My role in *Girl Crazy*, when I became a success, was handed to me on a silver platter. After that, I went into George White's *Scandals* and *Take a Chance*, and both of them helped me. So the way I figure it, Cindy's tale is a downbeat one compared to mine.

Take one little angle. Take the fact that I never had to study singing. All those little kids in the Bronx, with their mommas dragging them to singing schools and dancing schools—that never happened to me.

The way I get it, people make their own luck by putting out everything they've got, and the more they put out, the more luck they have. It may have been an accident that I was born a little girl with a big voice—the description of me I like best is "a doll from Astoria with a trumpet in her throat"—but ever since I was five I've been standing on my own hind legs and selling the voice I was born with for all I was worth.

If selling it is luck, then I've been lucky.

My philosophy is this: if you're able to develop yourself into a top performer at anything, face it bravely, sister. Admit it instead

33

of blushing prettily, twisting your apron, and scuffing your toe in the dust.

There was once a song about Lindbergh. It was called "Lucky Lindy"! To me, it was the biggest batch of applesauce ever cooked. Lindy was good, he knew his job, he concentrated on it; he was—and is—a pro. "Lucky" Lindy my foot!

It's hard for me to talk like this without sounding like a big operator in the "and then I wrote" department. This is a theatrical expression a certain kind of song writer uses. He's at a party, he sees a piano, and without waiting for anybody to ask him, he springs at that stool and plays one of his songs. Still with no urging from anybody, he says, "And then I wrote——" and he mentions the name of another of his songs and plays that one, too, ready or not.

And so he goes, on and on and on. That's where the expression came from—from those characters who sit down and play their whole repertoire. Nobody can stop them.

Well, I've got my own "and then I wrote" department. In it are such things as "Ethel Merman is fun to listen to, even for a man with a head cold," and "She can put over the Boy Scout oath in song or Article Four, Section One, of the Constitution." I wish I could remember the names of the two nice guys who said those things.

Then I love something Buddy De Sylva said: "Watching Merman in a show after she's got her lines and her songs and her stage business all set is like watching a movie after it's been filmed and edited. After that, no matter how many times you see it and hear it, it's always the same."

34

Buddy—God rest his soul—was the first to star me. He put my name up in lights on a marquee: ETHEL MERMAN IN PANAMA HATTIE. Previously I had always costarred. "You're ready," Buddy said. "There's no reason why you can't carry a show by yourself, like a suitcase." It was then that I got a load of the nice things that come with success. All of a sudden I had an ermine wrap, a mink coat, a broadtail and silver fox, and a dressing room right off the wings. In addition to furs and first-floor dressing room, I had a maid, an apartment in Central Park West, and a car and chauffeur.

I soon sold the car. It was in dead storage most of the time. Where can you go in New York anyway? I got rid of it, and I've never bought one since. I lived at 25 Central Park West, so I was close to anywhere I wanted to go. If I wanted to shop on Fifth Avenue, the walk across Central Park was good for me. With a car, there was no place to park, and my driver had to keep on going round and round the block. Usually I came out of a store just in time to see him whip by, and I'd have to wait thirty minutes for him to get around the block again. So I vetoed the whole deal and went in for walking or jumping into taxis. If it was a special occasion and I had on a long evening dress, particularly in the winter and I didn't want to mess up the dress on a wet cab floor, I'd hire a car and chauffeur.

In the end, it was a relief not to have that chauffeur and car hanging around. Anyhow, that jockey wore out three clutches in a year. He was clutch-happy. He did what hackies and truckers called "riding the clutch." Every time he breathed, voom! he used it.

35

I keep the various attempts people have made at analyzing my voice in my "and then I wrote" collection too. I've collected a lot of those descriptions and comparisons, or whatever. Some of them are amusing, some interesting, some I don't dig at all. I'll toss in a few. It's been said that I can hold a note as long as the Chase National Bank. I wouldn't know about the Chase, but I do hold one pretty long. I held a middle C, in "I Got Rhythm," for sixteen bars. I began with the second chorus of "I Got Rhythm," only instead of singing, I made an *"Ah-h-h-h"* sound and held it. The band played the melody, and I held the note over it.

This didn't require any training in breathing and stomach control. I just took a breath and held it. God gave me my voice, and it's always been on hand, loud and brassy, when I needed it.

I don't know whether Toscanini's remark about me is an item for any collection or not. See how you figure it. Buck Crouse was eager to know what a good, solid musician thought of my voice. He knew Sam Chotzinoff, who was a great friend of Toscanini. He was talking to him one night and Sam said he wanted to see a show I was in, and Buck asked, "Do you suppose the Toscaninis would like to see the show too? The tickets will be on me."

"They'd love to," Sam said. "Why?"

"I'd like to find out what he thinks of Ethel's pipes," Buck said.

Chotzy told Buck later that the maestro listened to my first number, "I Get a Kick Out of You," with a puzzled look on his face; then turned to Chotzy and said, *"Castrato!"*—a word which meant the best qualities of a female voice mixed with a masculine voice.

When this was first repeated to me, I was snowed, but it was explained to me that in Italy, in the old days, to get the perfect voice for grand opera or for a church choir, they hunted around until they'd found singers who sounded like grown-up choir boys. The way I get it, Toscanini was saying that my voice has a double-sexed quality.

He also said, "Hers is not a human voice. It's another instrument in the band." As for the instrument Toscanini mentioned—it's a Merman horn. I've been blowing it since I was five. Walter Winchell put it another way. He said I was born with a silver tune in my mouth.

Somebody else—not Toscanini—said, "Merman's voice has the hard forthrightness of a jazz trumpet—an ability to stay on pitch while she shouts at the top of her lungs." Another critic said—and I think this one ordinarily covered the Met—"She has a big, well-focused contralto. You might say it goes on a straight line." I've tried many times to figure out what he meant. I guess he meant, "She's on key."

As for "well-focused," I've never heard of that. It must be a long-hair expression.

At the end of his take-out on me, this same guy broke down and said, "Hell, it's quite an organ. It's got ping. I guess she's got leather down there."

There's no doubt that my vocal cords are durable. They are also low-down and all alone by themselves. Whenever I felt my throat trouble coming on, I'd go to Dr. Stuart Craig, and he'd

dose me and pull me back in shape. I remember Dr. Craig saying, "I can't even see your vocal cords. They must be somewhere
down in your calves." So I get the picture that mine are different
from everybody else's, at least in where they're placed.

I've got another notion you'd better check on with a doctor
yourself, but I've worked it out that if you've got virus X and you
go to work anyhow, you're doing yourself a favor. Suppose you
stay home when you're sick, and they put all kinds of things in
you and on you to make you perspire. Well, all you have to do is
one performance of *Call Me Madam* and you're perspiring. That
way you get rid of a lot of poison in your system and you feel
better.

Going from tonsils to tenses, I've talked a lot so far about the
Levitts, but it's been in the past tense. Now I'm married to a guy
named Bob Six, and it's about time I was getting to the present
tense and talking about the Sixes. I won't tell how I met him;
that'll come later, when I get to clicking this off on a more or less
year-to-year basis. But I want to make it plain right now that I'm
happy the way I am. I liked Six the minute I met him, but I tried
not to let him know it. For one thing, I didn't think I was interested in getting married again. I'd been married a long time
and had had two children. But, not to be girlish about it, I found
I was crazy about Six and, after I got to know him, I prayed that
we'd get together someday, although I knew he lived in Denver.
I love my father and my mother very much, and when I married
Bob Six and went to Denver, leaving the town where my parents
live was the big decision. I considered it for a long time. But once
I made up my mind, that was it.

The nice thing about Six is that he's not a wise guy the way Broadway means the term. He's something more important than that; he's an adult. He's a nice, big, easygoing guy who's wonderful to me. He makes me feel young and beautiful, and in case you didn't know it, that does plenty for a woman. When I'm dressed up to go out, he'll say, "My, you look nice." If a man puts out a kind word like that once in a while, brother, that's quite a man. If he tells me that he doesn't like me in a dress, I won't wear it; it takes all the fun out of it. I may wear it again, to lunch with the girl friends, but I don't wear it with him.

It's funny, when I talk to old friends, like Irving Berlin and Dorothy Fields, or Arthur Schwartz, or Howard Lindsay and Buck Crouse, one and all they refuse to believe that I won't be back working in another Broadway show with them someday. When I say, "But I'm not coming back to New York," somebody mentions the fact that Bob Six travels a lot. "Yes," I say, "he's gone for two days, three days, maybe more, but that's not the kind of separation it would be if I were in a New York show that ran two or three years, the way *Annie* did, while my husband is knocking around in Denver. I like the kind of life I lead now, because when Bob has to go away, I'm free to go with him. What's more, he *wants* me to go with him. If I were in a New York show, I couldn't do it."

I know people say, "If you don't like being married to a self-sufficient woman you're out of luck when you marry Merman." I don't agree with that. I may be self-sufficient, but I rely on Bob Six tremendously. I ask for his opinion on so many things and I value it when he gives it to me. To tell you the truth, I'm hungry for somebody to lean on when I'm bushed—and I don't mean just physically.

I'll give you another clue. Everybody wants security, but to a woman security is not just money. After all, Hetty Green had that, and how happy was she? Security is also a husband who thinks you're swell, a home, kids.

I'm very happy with Six. This guy is great for me. He loves my friends and he loves the theater, but first of all he's a businessman. Not only do I have somebody I'm in love with, but I have a man who's interested in my work and my business. The only thing he's ever asked of me is, "Please don't use any four-letter words in front of other people."

It seemed a reasonable request.

Suppose I did go back to Broadway and do a show. The way the income-tax setup is now, if a show runs a year and a half, after the first four months the money I make out of it belongs to the government. In the meantime, since I'm a star who's interested in her job and I never slough a performance, afternoon or evening, I'm knocking my brains out. Matinee days are rough; two shows a day really drain a girl.

What I'd like to do is work in one picture a year, take on about four television dates, and have my home life too. That way I won't be tied down and I can travel with Six when he travels. Besides, with a movie a year and a few TV shows, you've got something different going all the time.

It's not much to ask. I'm only asking to have my cake and eat it too.

I've been told that writing your autobiography should be like curling up on a head-shrinker's couch while he makes with the pencil and notebook. They say that the big idea in telling your story is to tell it so the people who read it will know you when they've finished it. The things you think about, the things that happen to you, the way you feel about those things when they happen all add up to being you.

Chapter Three

I know that sooner or later I'll have to get around to the stale routine which begins: "I was born on such-and-such a day in such-and-such a place." But I'm going to put that off as long as I can. By the time I get to it you'll know more about what kind of a dame I am.

I have a set of rules and I try to live up to them. When I sign a contract, I figure it's my duty to give the best I've got. My employers have a right to expect that of me. I don't care how much work there is, or how late I stay, or how many costumes I have to fit—I do it if it's for the good of the show. But if somebody tries to take advantage of me, I speak my piece in what I hear is Anglo-Saxon. Those Anglos and Saxons must not have pulled their punches.

Maybe it's a childlike quality, but when I'm mad I let you know I'm mad, and when I'm happy I let you know I'm happy. I don't hold anything back. I can yell loud, but I don't go in for three- or four-day sulks.

I believe in theater etiquette. I have the greatest respect for the one who's boss. In other words, forty other fellows can tell me what's what but I'll still ask the producer, "What do you think?" because I know that only the boss is right. Right or wrong, he's right. Any other way, you've got a mess.

I have no time for unprofessionals. I try to be a pro myself and I only like dealing with pros. In other words, if I don't know a person's quality, he's got to prove himself to me. If you walked in with a fellow and said to me, "This is the greatest living writer," I'd say, "Yeah? What has he written? Let me read it." But once I'm convinced you're good, I'm your girl.

Some of my other habits are these: I have my fun, I have my drinks (champagne on the rocks, in a tall glass), but I also get plenty of rest, and tomorrow morning at seven-thirty on the set I'll be ready. I'll know my part and everyone else's part. I've never left a show in my life once it has opened. I stick right with them until the producers decide to close them in New York. That's why I've been in comparatively few shows in my long career in show business. I've had one vacation in all that time, a month off during the run of *Annie Get Your Gun*, which had run for two years. When I came back I picked it up and stayed another year with it.

I try to have a great deal of patience, and I play ball with you so determinedly that a few birdbrains have even called me "grimly co-operative." But it's not hard to be patient and co-operative when you have a sense of your own security. Only the insecure are impatient and cranky.

Not that I don't protect myself at all times. When I'm working with other performers, we shake hands, go to our corners, and come out determined not to hit low, rabbit-punch, or butt, but at the same time we keep our dukes up—just in case. I'm nice, but I know every trick of the trade, such as upstaging or jumping on the other fellow's lines. I'm up there on the stage or before the camera to be seen, and I see to it that I am!

"Jumping on a line" means this: you read your speech before the other actor comes to the period at the end of his line. It's really a form of interrupting. You can protect yourself against it by coming right back and doing the same thing to the line-jumper. Instead of being offended and sulking, just step up the line-jumping pace until the other character gets tired of trying to start his lines before you finish yours.

There's a belief in some quarters that I am one of the symbols of Broadway; that I'm the kind of girl who's never traveled west of the George Washington Bridge, spiritually. I'll take this up later along with the crack one "friend" made: "I think that any man Ethel marries must know before he signs the papers that her work will always be more important to her than anything else, except her children. . . . Whoever marries her, unless he's a gutsy guy, is going to finish second to the stage and screen."

For right now, all I'll say is to repeat a remark by Cole Porter: "It's fun to watch the Sixes. They have a good time together. They laugh together."

To get back to getting to know me: I'm definite. I have no flossiness. I tend to business. I try to be a clean, wholesome gal but one who knows where she is going and what the score is and

44

who is unstuffy and can laugh or tell a joke with the best of them.

Among odd facts about me are: The one time when I insisted on complete relaxation when I was in a show was during dinner. I turned off my phone from six to seven. That was my time. And I've always loved dogs. Aside from my children and my husband, dogs have been the love of my life. I even like pictures of dogs, and miniatures of dogs on my mantelpiece.

I've never done any gambling. I never bet on horses, for instance. That's not my idea of being smart. I was never flighty and giddy; I was never interested in bright young playboys. I've always preferred the steady businesslike lads.

I try to be completely prepared for everything I run into. If it's possible for me to know that I'm going to encounter a thing, I prepare for it thoroughly. Even if it's only a cocktail party where I know I'll be asked to sing, I prepare my songs especially in advance. If I say, "I'll call you at twelve," I call at twelve on the minute. If I say, "I'll meet you at one for luncheon," one o'clock I'm there. I'm always on time.

I've been told that I'm an unexpected combination of expertness and hot-stuff party gal. The latter are usually all one way; no efficiency at all. But I'm not only a good businesswoman, I'm a good housekeeper too. Still, when I walk in all dressed up in diamonds and furs, I don't think you'd ever think that this is a gal who does her own pin curls, who goes down and looks in the icebox, and if the stuff isn't covered or the coils haven't defrosted, she'll do it herself. Or that I'm a girl who, when she fires the help, will get down and scrub the kitchen floor. I've not only done it but I've done it better than the help I fired.

45

When it comes to keeping myself ready for work I've got a will of iron. I can be very strict with myself. Some dames are a real bore about their rules and regimes for themselves. Me, I'm quietly strict about them. I have my rules and I stick to them, and nothing can change me, but I don't sound off about them all the time.

When people ask me how I got the way I am, I say I don't know—unless it's because I give everything I've got to anything I go into. Some days I feel bum, other days good, but I don't vary. I don't let down. I don't ask anybody to do anything at a rehearsal I won't do. I'll stay later than anybody. I won't let the chorus kids outwork me.

One thing that makes me different from most people in show business is, I don't have a case of nerves opening night. The producers and directors, the actors and actresses with whom I've worked think that amazing. I don't think it's amazing. Why should I be nervous? Those people out front came to see me; I didn't come to see them. They were the ones who paid their dough to be entertained. I didn't. Since they are risking their dough, I figure they were the ones who ought to be jumpy. I tell myself, *If they could do what I'm doing any better than I can, they'd be up here on the stage and I'd be out there in a seat.* They tell me that I must be a phenomenon because everybody gets nervous. Some actors and actresses have to go to the bathroom five or six times before they go on.

The afternoon after the opening of *Annie Get Your Gun*, Levitt brought home the evening papers. They carried wonderful reviews of the show, but I hadn't bothered to buy them. The way I look at reviews, if they're good, they're good, and if they're bad, they're bad. All a performer should care about is knowing inside herself that she's done a good job. You can't make a critic praise you by just wanting him to.

When Levitt came home and said, "Oh boy, look at these reviews!" I was sitting at my bedroom desk, checking the grocery bills.

I said, "Good grief! Peaches have jumped three cents more a can than they were last week."

Levitt never got over that. There he was, with those great notices, and me worrying about peaches hiking up three cents. It was a side of me he didn't get. He never did get it.

After six months of being in a Broadway show, there are nights when you think it'll kill you if you go through the same routine again. The audience looks the same. Their faces are the same. You begin to think that the part of the theater you can see is never emptied; the people have never gone home. You put the same effort into it. You belt the songs over with the same sock, but it becomes mechanical.

I've watched my favorite pianist, Lew Kessler, in the pit during many's the big show. He sits there, looking over the house, casing the audience, and playing a beautiful piano. But Lew told me, "After one of my shows has been running for months, sometimes I look down at the music on my rack and I've played five numbers without knowing it."

After a show has been running for a spell, I can be out there singing a song and thinking, *Little Ethel should go for a haircut tomorrow. I have to go downtown and get so-and-so and so-and-so.*

47

The first thing I know, the number's over, and I've planned my whole day.

Lew and I call those people who look as if they'd never gone home "the Dogs." A Dog is somebody who doesn't laugh or clap. He just sits. He's bought his tickets at the Dog Ticket Agency or he's got in touch with a Dog speculator and has forked over twenty-five dollars a seat. He's sore because he's had to pay twenty-five bucks, so he wants twenty-five dollars' worth of blood, and no matter what he's got, he doesn't think it's twenty-five dollars' worth.

The Dogs are the ones you see from the stage, reflected in the stage lights. They always come late because, having paid so much, they want to take out part of their value making an entrance and being noticed.

Helen Hayes told me a funny thing once. She said that she'd been in one play such a long time that she had gotten into the habit of thinking about other things while delivering her lines. Once she woke up to the fact that she was thinking and not delivering any lines at all. She'd gone blank. I've never had that happen to me. I was glad she told me about it. Warned is warned.

Lew Kessler knows me pretty well, and he says of me, "Mermo's always been a girl who'd rather have a rhinestone orchid than two tickets to *Faust*."

He's right. I just love nice jewelry. I love it because I've worked like a horse to get it. But I can still kid myself about it. I point to a big chunk of it on me and ask, "What do you think of the door knocker, kid?"

It was the kick of the world when I got my name up in lights. Then I decided that I wanted to see my name in another kind of lights. TV may have its color spectaculars, but I have my own. During each show I've bought myself a big wad of jewelry to remember the production by. Once I bought a bracelet of two parallel rows of rubies an inch apart, with "Ethel A. Merman"—A. for Agnes—spelled in diamonds between the two rows. The name is in matched baguettes. It took six months to make it up. I wear it to special parties when I'm all gussied up.

I've never gone into my story before with as much detail as I'm going into it here. In the past I've threatened to type out stock interviews, have copies made, hand them out, and say, "You take it from here, boys."

I remember I once went through an interview sparring session with Robert Garland, an ace reporter of the *Journal-American*. According to Garland, I asked, "Which interview do you want?"

"Which interview have you got?" Garland asked.

"There're the old reliable three," I told him. "There's the sure-shot Merman, in which I've never had a failure; there's the 'doing what comes naturally' one, in which I revamp the story of my overnight success with 'I Got Rhythm,' in *Girl Crazy*; and there's the mother and the homebody one in which I loathe the country and love the city."

There was nothing phony about any of these, but I was so fed up with interviews that I felt like kidding about them.

"I've used them all," Garland told me.

"So has everybody else," I said, "and with pop-up pix. Or I

can give you the 'I don't think I'll ever cut off my topknot' one, or the one in which I discard the Zim—the first three letters of my real name—and the last *n* and emerge as Merman."

If I were bobbing and weaving around the ring with Garland now, I'd tell him, "I've got a new one, the 'I'm crazy about Denver' one, and 'They'll never get me back to the old Broadway treadmill.' " And this time I wouldn't be kidding either.

Those who know me know that there are two Ethel Mermans. There's Merman the entertainer; and Merman the practical housekeeper, zealous mother and dame who was one of the first to use a washing machine. I admit I'm hip to what's going on in my house. (Hip is hep in spades; it means I'm more *au courant* than anybody.)

I know where everything is. I know every nook and corner. I go around with a pinky sticking out, touching the tops of picture frames, window sills, and furniture. If there's dust there, I know it.

I'm content to leave the effectiveness of Merman the entertainer to others. My success at this dodge is a matter of opinion. I'll string along with the girl who, when the house detective asked her, "Are you entertaining a gentleman in your room?" said, "Just a minute. I'll ask him."

Part of my philosophy is not to avoid facts. This includes the facts of life. I think they're natural and normal. I don't sneer at 'em or leer at 'em. I don't mind earthy humor as long as it's healthy humor. Sometimes I shock people with a thigh-slapping, locker-room-type joke and sometimes I startle them with what they think is prudery.

To me, sex has its funny aspects. It can even be gay. I try to make others feel the same way about it.

Even so, I'm not the type dame whose big trick is selling sex on the stage. Can you imagine trying to sell sex in some of the outfits I've worn? Take the black cotton stockings, the moccasins, and the saggy buckskin skirt I wore as Annie Oakley, with a couple of dead quail hung around my waist. I dare you to sell sex in that outfit. If you can, I know where you can get some attractive offers.

I've never been dirty in my life. Earthy, yes; but not dirty. I'm a dame who can take a naughty situation and make it seem as plain and natural as bread and butter. At least, I've been told that I can. Kids watch me in the theater and, whether they understand my jokes or not, they usually laugh, and kids never laugh at anything that's wrong or dirty. They're very sensitive that way.

When I lived in New York, I attended St. Bartholomew's Episcopal Church. My former husband, Bob Levitt, got to be quite a guy at St. Bartholomew's. They even had him taking up the collection. Levitt used to complain that it always seemed that he was suffering from a hangover while passing the plate because, when I was in a show, Saturday nights were the only times we two could go out on the town and stay up late. Not only did he have to pass the plate hung over, but our pew was in the fifth row, in front of the pulpit, so the Levitts were always under the gun.

Chapter Four

I keep ringing in so much home life, I might as well tell about the first home I ever had. It was the top floor of my grandma's house at 359 Fourth Avenue in Astoria, Long Island. I was born there. Mom had to rush home from a wedding to be present when I arrived. It was not *her* wedding. Mom was at her best girl friend's wedding when she started to get pains and Pop took her home to Grandma's three-story house.

We lived on what you might call a private street. No one went through, no wagons or anything; just the people that lived there. I went over there about four or five years ago. It was terrible to see. It's all built up.

My grandmother's maiden name was Hunter. Her married name was Mary Gardner.

The house was a frame house. It had a large stoop that used to be a wooden one until my mother's father, who was in the building trade, made it into a concrete stoop with a front porch screened in in the summertime so we could sit out there without having to slap at the flies and mosquitoes. There was a sort of downstairs floor with steps running up to it from the sidewalk. It was rented out.

Next to my grandmother's house was another house and next to that was a lot. Beyond that was another house where my mother's older sister lived with her family. Her name was Margaret Sharkey. Next to Aunt Margaret's was an orchard with apple trees in it. Mom once had a picture of the two of us sitting underneath a tree in that orchard while I was wearing a very short dress with lace on the hem, lace sleeves, and a big bow.

My mother always dressed me in sashes with huge bows in the middle of my back, and she starched my dresses so stiff that they'd flatten out if I sat down. But I knew enough to hike my dresses up so they wouldn't wrinkle.

The dress I wore in the photo taken in the orchard had a box-pleated skirt. Mom bought it instead of making it herself. She always took me into New York for my dresses, and she bought my shoes at Coward's, which meant that they were good. "Never wear cheap shoes," Mom told me. "Your feet will pay for them if you do." I've followed her advice and I've never had any trouble with my feet to this day.

I'm Scots-German. Mom is Scots; Pop is German. It's not hard to tell that from his name, Zimmermann. Pop spells his name with two *n*'s, which seems to make a difference (I don't know why), and he's a Lutheran.

As far as religions go, the Zimmermanns are all mixed up. On

Memorial Day, my pop's brother's daughter's husband drives him out to the Lutheran cemetery to put flowers on his mother's and father's graves. My mother's family were mostly Presbyterians, and I was baptized and confirmed in the Episcopal Church, at the Church of the Redeemer, in Astoria.

When I was growing up I went to church three times every Sunday, plus Christian Endeavor on Sunday nights. That's quite a slug of church. And before I moved to Denver, I was very active in St. Bartholomew's Church on Park Avenue, in New York. As a matter of fact, I gave a couple of concerts in the Community Hall there to raise funds for the church and they went over O.K., she said modestly.

People say that I've got part of Pop in me and part of Mom, too. Mom is the one with the hard head and the shrewdness, the one who won't let anybody cheat her. Mom taught me all I know about housekeeping and, believe you me, I know how to keep house right! Pop's sweeter, the easygoing type. Mom springs quicker than Pop, but he's smart in his way. He thinks things out and when he's finished thinking them out he only goes one way— the right way. With him there's no in-between.

Before I married, if I had any problems I'd go to Pop and talk to him, and if I took his advice things turned out all right. The bigger things, I mean. I never discussed my girlish problems with him. That's why I wish I'd had a brother or a sister, because, when a couple of girls are only a few years apart, they talk to each other about going out and dates and stuff. There are things you never say to your parents like what should you have done when a certain boy friend tried to kiss you?

54

You gas with a sister about that, not with your mother. When I had my first baby I thought, *I'm not going to have her going through life an only child.* So I made up my mind to have a brother or sister for Little Ethel. Being an only child can be lonesome, I'm telling you.

Pop was and is an accountant for James H. Dunham & Co., wholesale dry goods, at 345 Broadway. I can't get him to quit. The first thing I remember is Pop playing the piano for me. He not only played for me, for more than twenty years. He was organist for the Astoria Advanced Lodge of Masons.

From the first my voice was easily identifiable. When I was a baby and people in the next room or down the street heard me, they'd say, "That's Ethel." I don't know where that voice of mine came from, because I've never had a lesson in my life.

Pop and Mom were proud of my voice and they didn't have to nip at my calves with a blacksnake whip to make me stand up before people and sing. I sang Sunday nights at the Lutheran Church and at Pop's Masonic lodge. And I sang for the Women's Republican Club of Astoria. Mom was president of that at one time.

Mom also ushered me around to perform for the World War I soldiers. I dressed in a plaid skirt and pulled my hat down over one eye to look tough for the tough little songs I sang, such as "He's Me Pal," which was the first song I remember singing in public. Mom always sat in the front row, and I dedicated the last verse of a song to her. It went like this: "Friends may be few and friends may be true, but I have one dear friend of old. Bless her dear heart, we will never part, for she loves me better than gold." Coming from a six-year-old, this made those dough-boys' tear ducts feel funny.

The effect was helped by the fact that when I was a little girl I wasn't inclined to be chubby. I was a very thin child. Mom tells me I wouldn't eat. Then somewhere along the way I had whooping cough. After that I had an appetite.

One Christmas I went out to Camp Yaphank and sang "Maggie Dooley" and "K-K-K-Katy," and "How Ya Gonna Keep 'Em Down on the Farm?" Some organization had made up knick-knack kits for the boys in the wrap-around puttees and the General-Pershing-type felt hats. One of those doughboys gave me his kit. It was a long time ago, but I still remember it. If I'd been a teen-age Brooklyn Mata Hari whose sweater showed off the fact that she had matured early, it would have been different, but to give a kit to a little kid, that was *something*.

Evenings, when it was dusk, we played games. One called potsy was like hopscotch. We made chalk marks on the sidewalk. Then we threw a pebble, and wherever it landed we had to skip over that place on the sidewalk. We also skipped rope, double Dutch. That meant with two ropes going at the same time. I was great at that, even if I was no good at rope-climbing and physical culture at school.

When I was little and going to public school, I'd come home afternoons and stand outside a movie studio in Astoria with a big wooden fence around it. When I was in a show called *Girl Crazy* I wound up at the same studio making shorts myself. It's a crazy world, ain't it? We kids used to go up there and look through the holes other kids had gouged in the fence's wooden palings, and watch them make movies. Then I'd wait for the movie stars to come out.

Word as to what days they'd be shooting behind that fence got around to every kid in the neighborhood. It was as if we had receiving sets in our heads. I wasn't responsible for gouging any of the holes in the fence, but I enjoyed looking through them. Whoever did it, I was thankful for them.

It may come as news to any young fry who read this that Paramount once owned that studio in Astoria. I think they called it the Jesse Lasky Studio or the Famous Players Studio then, but later both those names were rolled into one to become Paramount.

That was even before Crosby and Hope. It was even before Gary Cooper began making semitalking pictures. But I'd better not make it too far back in the gaslight period, because I was one of the kids who pushed an eyeball against a hole in that fence.

The great and the glamorous came to work in block-long cars shiny with nickel. And we neighborhood kids stood there, stiff with excitement, and watched. I never saw Valentino. I would have remembered him if I had. But I did see Greta Nissen, Adolphe Menjou, Gilda Gray, and, to me, the most beautiful of all, Alice Brady. She had a Japanese chauffeur who sat by himself up in front with a sheet of glass between him and Alice—the kind of glass partition you could crank up and down. I remember hers was a big black car. That was in the days when black meant class instead of a two-toned chassis and top with fluorescent color effects.

Watching her, I decided to be not only a singer but an actress too. The trouble was, I didn't think I'd ever be beautiful enough

57

to be an actress. Nobody had told me that beauty wasn't the only way to fame on the stage and what was then called "the silver screen." I would never be any raving beauty, but I wasn't going to be the ugliest person in the world either. When I'd reached the age bracket where I was getting testimonials from gentleman friends, I was told I was attractive and fun to have along. Now that I'm older—and if I'm not wiser I've wasted my time—I know that being attractive is better than being beautiful. To coin a saying, beauty doesn't last long, and attractiveness doesn't rub off easily.

In my Alice-Brady-worshiping period a man called Uncle Tom used to take me to the matinees at the Palace Theater in New York every other Sunday. He really wasn't my uncle, but Pop and Uncle Tom were pals. I saw all the big stars of the day—Nora Bayes and Grace La Rue and Blossom Seeley. Afterward I went home and tried to sing like the canaries I'd heard at the Palace. Funny thing, I ended up not singing like any of them. Then Mom took me instead of Uncle Tom and she took me on Friday nights instead of to Sunday matinees. There was no school on Saturdays and I could sleep in.

When it was time for me to go to William Cullen Bryant High School, located by the Bridge Plaza in Long Island City, Mom wanted me to take a general course and learn to be a schoolteacher. I wanted no part of that. I didn't want to be a schoolteacher. I wanted to be a singer. But I had enough ego not to want to fool around being a chorus or a show girl until something worth while to do on the stage came along. Until that happened, I thought I'd mark time as a stenographer. So I took the four-year commercial course, which included bookkeeping, short-hand, and typing. Typing has always fascinated me. I'm not bad at it right now.

The fact that I know how to take shorthand notes has been very helpful to me in the theatrical business, particularly during rehearsals. There might come a change in the script, a substituting of this line for that line, a switching something around, and I'd get mine down in the margin of the script in shorthand. Then I'd go home, type it out, and paste it over the old line.

This business of keeping all brushed up and ready to go with my stenography has inspired at least one tall tale. According to this story, I was flying East, and on my way to the airport I dropped in at a movie studio to sign an important document. No-body could find the contract and no stenographers were available so I grabbed a pad and pencil and made pothooks while the studio's legal lights dictated an important, big-money agreement. Then, switching from stenographer to star, I signed the paper and caught my plane. The only trouble with that story is that it never happened. It was a publicity plant. It must be, because I never did it.

But to be real honest about it, I've never had a secretary. I'm my own secretary. I answer everything myself, my bills and correspondence. If I get a note or a present, I sit down and acknowledge it in longhand.

When I graduated from Bryant I went to work in the office of the Boyce-ite Company on Queens Boulevard. Boyce-ite made an anti-freeze product. I stayed there for a while and I wasn't doing so dusty—I'd been promoted to the vice-president's office—

when I learned that the B. K. Vacuum Booster Brake Company was opening an office across the street.

The Boyce-ite employees ate in a nearby lunchroom and I met Vic Kliesrath there. He was the one who told me that the Bragg-Kliesrath Corporation was just forming, and that his partner, Caleb Bragg, needed a secretary. Bragg was president of the company.

According to Louis Shurr, who's Bob Hope's agent and Bert Lahr's agent, as well as an agent for many another important theatrical figure, Caleb Bragg was one of his best friends. Shurr vouches for the fact that Caleb Bragg invented one of the most successful automatic washing machines and that later on he went into the real estate business with Carl Fisher, who started to make Miami Beach popular.

Still later, Mr. Bragg built a unique home out at Montauk Point on Long Island. This house had six different units: each one consisting of a dining room, living room, bedroom, and kitchen; all joined together or all operating as individual units at his whim. Shurr says that along with Jules Glaenzer, who was vice-president of Cartier's, he used to visit Mr. Bragg. And Shurr also says that Mr. Bragg was a wonderful, wonderful man; very quiet, very subdued, very conservative, but that he always liked beautiful girls. He patronized a top tailor in New York and wore dark suits to work. He never overdressed. He was a gentleman to his finger tips. Well, that was Mr. Bragg: well known socially, and a great admirer of the theater and of beautiful girls. And he had this inventive mind which I guess he needed with all *those* interests.

I was drawing twenty-three dollars a week at Boyce-ite, but I made thirty-five at Bragg-Kliesrath. The B. K. Vacuum Booster Brake Company was a crazy name. People still asked me, "What's a booster brake, for God's sake?" I still tell them I don't know.

I can't blueprint it, but I do know that when I graduated from high school my mother gave me a car and Mr. Bragg and Vic Kliesrath put a B. K. vacuum booster brake on it. All I had to do was touch the brake pedal and voom, I stopped on a dime. I guess boosters put pressure on the brakes or something. The first time I tried it, I nearly went through the windshield. However, the B. K. vacuum booster brakes were mostly for tractors and trucks.

Vic Kliesrath was the technical one. He'd get an idea for a new patent; then he or Mr. Bragg would dictate the technical stuff to me.

They didn't dictate quickly but the phrases they used were out of my sphere. Mechanical terms, stuff like that. All the various parts of motors and what not. And they dictated I don't know how many pages. I'd type it all out and it would be sent to Louis Prevost Whitaker, the firm's patent attorney. If I didn't know what Kliesrath or Mr. Bragg was talking about, I left out the technical stuff.

Occasionally Mr. Bragg read my letters back and asked me with a puzzled air, "Didn't I give you more than this?"

"Sure, Mr. Bragg," I'd say, "but they didn't teach us that stuff in high school. We just got ordinary language, like people talk."

Mr. Bragg looked at me with a dazed look. Then in longhand he'd insert what I'd left out, sign it, and send it out that way.

I didn't have to type it over again. Although I bobbled the technical gibberish, I handled the rest of his mail O.K.

I hadn't been with Mr. Bragg very long before I found out he had important friends in the theater—producers and actors, but mostly actresses. I was interested in this theatrical side of Mr. Bragg, for by this time I'd listed my name with agents who supplied talent for private parties and small affairs.

You signed their registers and indicated what you did, such as: "Singer—Blues." Then if they needed any they called you.

I never called Mr. Bragg anything but Mister. But I got to know Kliesrath, the vice-president, and his wife very well. He had a lovely home at Port Washington. I'd go out to visit them on Saturday nights and, if they had a party going, they'd have a small orchestra in and I'd sing what was popular. But Mr. Bragg always held himself aloof. Not that he meant to be that way. He just couldn't help it.

My desk and Mr. Bragg's desk were in the same office, so I overheard his conversations when he called his butler to tell him, "So-and-so is coming for dinner." (He'd mention Gertrude Lawrence, or Irene Delroy, or George White, or Earl Carroll.) "Have something special."

I used to think, *If I could just meet those people and sing for them, they'd go for me. I know they would.*

One of my big moments was the day I went on a company picnic at Port Washington. Mr. Bragg's houseboat, the *Masquerader*, was lying off Port Washington, but we weren't invited on board. Mr. Bragg didn't make social contacts with anybody connected with the firm. Out of the office you'd have thought he didn't know one of us from the other. Still, since his employees were out there having a picnic and all, he did invite three or four of us for a ride on one of his speedboats.

We went almost to the Connecticut shore; then, coming back, we hit a chunk of wood and capsized. We were fished out and were taken on board Mr. Bragg's houseboat and our clothes were put in a fireless cooker to dry. Mr. Bragg lent us silk pajamas to wear while our stuff was baking, and promised to reimburse us for the damage we'd suffered. But, while that was important, the important thing to me was that Ruth Selwyn and her husband Edgar Selwyn, a big stage producer, were on board. We all sat down to a fabulous dinner.

I told Mrs. Selwyn who I was, that I worked for Mr. Bragg, and that I sang.

"That's nice," she said. Full stop.

I could see her thinking, *If her singing is any good, why is she a stenographer?* So talking to Ruth Selwyn didn't hurry my appearance on the stage.

What with entertaining at night, sometimes I was a little tired when I got to the office in the morning, so I'd knock off a nap in the ladies' room until Mr. Bragg came to work. He spent his winters in Palm Beach and summers on his boat. He was always taking off for Europe, or for Florida, or Lake Placid, or Pinehurst, or Tuxedo or some place like that. He'd come to work on a Tuesday, open his mail, and go back to his boat at Port Washington on Thursday. Even if he came to the office from his New York apartment (where he lived when he wasn't in Florida or on his boat) he didn't get there early. Ten or ten-thirty was his speed.

When I began to work club dates, this was a break for me. As I've said, mornings after a club date I'd be a little sleepy and I'd take off my dress, hang it up neatly on a hanger, and go to sleep until Mr. Bragg arrived. When that happened, one of the girls rushed into the ladies' room and warned me by saying "Chickee!" which was the same as saying, "Cheese it, the cops!" Then I'd put on my dress, and by the time Mr. Bragg had his hat off, I was strolling toward my desk with a letter in my hand.

The B. K. Vacuum Booster Brake Company shop took up almost the whole top floor of a two-story building. Downstairs was the Etched Products Corporation, so it was called the EPCO building. We were at the second elevated station on the elevated line, but the actual equipment for manufacturing the brakes was right outside the offices and, with those machines going all day, the noise was terrific. To compete with the racket, the telephone operator had a buzzer that rang a gong to summon various persons. Mr. Bragg got three gongs, the head of the purchasing department got four gongs. I got eight, so in addition to the shout of "Chickee," I'd hear private signal BONG-BONG-BONG-BONG-BONG-BONG-BONG-BONG when the operator saw Mr. Bragg coming.

Noontimes I hitched across the Queensboro Bridge with another secretary. I remember one day my girl friend and I were standing on the corner of Queens Boulevard hoping for a lift, since that was a quicker way of getting there, and otherwise we'd have to walk a couple of blocks to the el station and wait for a train, which would have taken up some of our lunch hour. Of course, if Mr. Bragg wasn't in town, it didn't make much difference. No one else kept tabs on me and I'd come back when I pleased, but when he was on deck it was different.

This particular day a big, long black car with the top down came along. It stopped for us and we climbed in. We said, "Gee! This is great." Then we looked down and there, under us and on the floor, were a lot of thorns, leaves, and stray blossoms. The driver was coming back from a funeral where he'd delivered a load of flowers. If we hadn't wanted to save time, we'd have hopped out. As it was, we stayed put.

When we got to New York we went over to Bloomingdale's at Fifty-ninth and Lexington and window-shopped. We might even buy a scarf. Then we'd go to a counter where they had wonderful tuna fish salad or crab meat sandwiches, gulp those in a hurry, and take the subway back. Big deal!

I got to thinking about how Mr. Bragg knew Earl Carroll and George White, the producer of the *Scandals*, until I could think of little else. Finally I grabbed my courage in both hands and said to Mr. Bragg, "I have a voice and I think I can sing. Hows about giving me a letter of introduction to George White?"

It is show-business legend that Mr. Bragg said to me, "Go ahead and write it yourself," and I wrote the letter of introduction myself, and he signed it. This is not true. Mr. Bragg dictated the letter and I transcribed it on my typewriter.

I didn't ask Mr. Bragg if I could have the afternoon off. I went to White's office after hours. We quit at five, and I made it over to White's office in the Apollo Theater Building on Forty-second Street between Broadway and Eighth Avenue at five-thirty.

The whole thing was over in five minutes. I didn't even get

into his office. He came out into an outer vestibule to talk to me. I gave him the letter, and he asked, "What do you do?"

I said, "I sing."

"Anyone who sings in my show must have a name," he said, "and I've already got a name—Frances Williams. She's starring in my new *Scandals*. However, I'll be happy to give you a job as a show girl."

He was busy and I was wasting his time, so I said, "Thank you," and left. I was very discouraged. I thought, *If a letter like that one from Mr. Bragg doesn't do it, I'm dead.*

Down around the Palace Theater the agents and the singers and others who wanted jobs entertaining all gathered. It was a kind of clearinghouse. There was a building there called the Bond Building, next door to the Palace, and a lot of agents holed up there too. You didn't have to sign a contract with an agent like that. Any agent who could get you a spot was your boy. But it got around among these agents that I was a pretty fair singer and pretty soon I had four or five of them booking me for club dates, although I was still working for Caleb Bragg.

A short time after that, one of the free-lancing agents I'd been doing jobs for around New York signed me to work a joint called the Little Russia, near Sixth Avenue on Fifty-seventh Street; at 100 West Fifty-seventh Street to be exact. It was down in a cellar. There was just the one show a night and that one went on after midnight. I only had to sing three or four songs. I don't know exactly what kind of food the place served because I never ate there, but I guess it specialized in Russian dishes. I only took the job for two weeks, at sixty bucks a week. I still kept my job with

66

Bragg and Kliesrath, so you might say I was working both sides of the street.

I didn't have to audition. They just needed a singer, and it made no difference whether I was good, bad, or indifferent. They didn't expect Tetrazzini for sixty dollars a week. I just went over there and sang. Period.

People didn't pay much attention to the entertainment at the Little Russia. It was mostly a place for eating and the customers just came in for an after-the-theater snack in a Russian atmosphere. The Little Russia wasn't a place where you had to be great. I was just someone up there singing from ten until one at night, while people kept on eating. I sang over their talking. There were a lot of places in New York where they supplied strictly non-sensational acts, doing non-show-stopping numbers along with the food and drink. Anyway, the Little Russia was where I got my start.

Chapter Five

The next thing I knew, an agent named Lou Irwin dropped in to the Little Russia, heard me sing, and signed me up. Two days later I went over to his office with Mom. Since I was under age, I had to have her to O.K. the contract.

It happened this way: One night I had finished my show at the Little Russia and was getting ready to go home when a waiter brought a card. Engraved on it was "Lou Irwin, Theatrical Representative." The waiter said the owner of the card wanted to speak to me. I said, "O.K." and Irwin told me that he thought I had possibilities as a singer. It was a favorable sign that Lou saw things in me. He's an astute agent, with a sharp eye for talent.

Lou himself describes all this in a lot more detail. He says that he was walking from Broadway and Fifty-seventh toward Fifth Avenue, on his way back from the opening of a show at the Guild Theater. His date for the evening was a little lady from California. At Fifty-seventh at the corner of Sixth he noticed that a low-ceilinged basement spot, the Little Russia, had opened. The doorman was a big fellow who stood six feet six and his name was Kuznitzoff. Later Kuznitzoff became an important Russian entertainer around New York and in Florida and other places. He was a baritone singer who played the accordion. He was wearing Russian regalia and a group of friends of the management and others were standing in front of the place. One of these lads imported and sold perfume to Flo Ziegfeld. He'd met Lou Irwin in Ziegfeld's office.

Ziegfeld loved to give gifts to the girls in his shows. You might almost say it was a hobby with him. He was always buying wonderful novelty gifts by the gross, to give away at parties. He never gave away trash. This guy who sold Flo perfume happened to see Lou and said to him, "Why don't you drop in? Some of my friends own this place; they're putting on entertainment and you ought to look it over." Lou asked the little girl with him if she'd like to stop in for some vodka and caviar, and she said jokingly, "Naturally I don't drink and naturally I don't care about caviar, but if they have corned beef and cabbage I'd love it." A kidder, that girl.

So they went in and had supper.

After a while I came out and sang "Moanin' Low," the song Libby Holman introduced in the first *Little Show*. Lou says now that I had a quality in my voice that he liked. Among other things it was loud and he could hear the words and understand them. So he sent for me and I came over to his table. When he asked me how long I'd been singing I said, "This is my first real engagement." And I told him about working daytimes as a secretary to Caleb Bragg.

Lou asked me to come to see him the next day and bring Mom or Pop with me, since I was under age. Mom and I went over after working hours, and we made a deal with Lou to represent me for nine years.

A couple of days later Lou arranged for me to meet Archie Mayo, a top movie director who was under contract to Warner Brothers. Then I auditioned for Lewis Warner, Harry Warner's son, and I signed a Warner contract with a six months' option clause, at a hundred and twenty-five dollars a week. Whether I worked or didn't work, I was to get that much each week. It was then that I decided to give up my job with Bragg and Kliesrath. Vic was sorry to see me go and Mr. Bragg wished me luck.

But although Warner Brothers had signed me, they didn't know what to do with me. Then somebody had the idea that, having signed a girl singer, it would be a bright notion if I wrapped my charms up in a leopard skin and raced across the stage at the Warner Avenue J studio in Brooklyn, in a jungle short subject, acting as a mechanical rabbit for a posse of hard-breathing cannibals or animals—I forget which.

You'd think that skipping around in a leopard skin in what I laughingly called "the movies," and getting a hundred and twenty-five bucks a week for being a potential starlet (at least, that's the way I thought of myself), I'd be happy as a cricket. The truth is, it was very frustrating. Even with pay checks coming in nothing was happening. I wasn't doing any work, so I began to get itchy and mentally tap my foot. I wanted to be singing. For the first time it dawned on me that if somebody paid you to do nothing it could be a pain in the neck. Up until then I'd figured such a life would be the nuts.

I appeared in one jungle-type short for Warner Brothers, but I don't think it ever saw a screen. I was dressed in a leather sarong and I sang a song with a lot of tom-toms booming behind me. Even while I was making it I thought: *No one will ever have the gall to show this on a screen.* It was awful.

Nobody cared whether I really worked or not. Nobody but me. I cared. So I went to Lou Irwin and Lou Irwin went to Warners, and they finally agreed to let me out so I could take outside singing jobs. It was November 1929, and a trio, Clayton, Jackson, and Durante, had been signed to appear at a brand-new night club on Broadway, Les Ambassadeurs. Lou heard that they needed a girl singer and he arranged for Clayton, who was the business manager of the threesome, to listen to me and look me over.

Jimmy Durante and Lou Clayton auditioned me and accepted me immediately. I was the singing personality in the show. There was a line of girls and I chirped a couple of numbers in front of the line. Not pop songs but songs written for the revue, so they'd fit in with what the girls were dancing. Then I did a pop song or two, like "Body and Soul" and "I've Got a Feeling I'm Falling."

For costumes I wore evening dresses. The club supplied dresses for the numbers I did in front of the line, but I had to supply my other dresses myself. But I couldn't afford anything too flossy so I guess my gowns weren't such a much. I remember one of them was a plain black chiffon with a big full skirt and a Bertha collar.

71

Another was a black satin dress. Neither of them was very elaborate and I was unhappy about that because at that point my idea of class was frills, bows, and furbelows. I've calmed down now, but that used to be my idea. You learn by experience.

Then I got a very bad throat; I was so sick I couldn't work, and had to leave. In January 1930 I had my tonsils removed. It broke my heart, but I had no alternative. I was getting two hundred dollars at the club, but that wasn't why I felt so bad about powdering. I'd gotten to know Jimmy, who's a real swell guy.

After the tonsillectomy I couldn't go back to work for a while, but singing instructors began coming around and telling me they could make a great star out of me if I'd take lessons, and it made me nervous. I wondered whether my voice was right or not. I began to lose sleep and weight, and have circles under my eyes. But I finally decided to forget it. I could always type, couldn't I?

Could be, having my tonsils chopped out had a permanent effect on my voice and made it louder. They had to go in so deep for my tonsils they severed a couple of blood vessels and I had to be sewed up. When I was convalescent Lou Irwin booked me into the Roman Pools Casino in Miami Beach, Florida. Two friends of his—John Steinberg and a man named Christo—operated the place. I worked there for six or seven weeks at three hundred dollars per. When the Florida season was over, I came home and teamed up with a piano player named Al Siegel. He knew all the blues-singing dodges, and he gave me some pointers. He made arrangements for me, we rehearsed, and I sang what he gave me to sing. But for the most part I followed my own rules.

When we got an act together we started out good. Siegel and I broke in at the Ritz Theater in Elizabeth, New Jersey, and *Variety* reported "a new singing team has come into existence with interesting arrangements by Siegel. And the girl can sing."

Al didn't sing. He was at the piano. Together we played some vaudeville engagements. In a 1934 interview I was quoted as saying, "I'd never played on the stage before and I didn't know anything about handling myself behind footlights. But after the first performance it was fun. I was singing blues and liking it, and so were the audiences. I couldn't ask for more out of life than that."

One newspaper writer gave a little of Al's previous history when he wrote, "Al had been married to a girl named Bee Palmer, whom he had transferred from a shimmy-shaker into a headliner. He married her only to have his romance wrecked on Broadway shoals."

Al Siegel had just returned from Europe and had separated from Bee, who was probably the greatest singer of popular songs the country had known up to that time. She was the first performer to ever take a classical song and sing it in rhythm style. Her salary at that time was said to be two thousand a week, which would be equal to ten thousand dollars or more today. But Bee didn't seem to care too much about working and quit. She was a stunning woman and could have gone to even greater heights because she had so much to offer.

When Al and Bee broke up, he came back to New York and Lou Irwin got him a booking as the leader of a four-piece combo orchestra in a little place on Fifty-second Street. Al played piano and led the orchestra. He had once worked in the orchestra that

73

accompanied Sophie Tucker; five men called the Five Kings of Syncopation.

Anyhow Al was free to work with me and my big, pounding voice was right down his street. Lou Irwin arranged for us to play some restaurants and clubs around New York City, and finally, in the summer of 1930, we were booked into the Brooklyn Paramount.

It was about then that I decided to change Zimmermann to Merman. I didn't think they'd ever get Zimmermann up in lights. It was too long. But I had to go through quite a thing with Pop about the change. He was dead against it. I wanted to take my mother's name—her name was Gardner—or my grandmother's name, Hunter, but Pop wouldn't hear of it. "If my name is good enough for me, it's good enough for you," he said. "Anyhow, it's your name."

"If I use part of it, will that be all right?" I asked, and reluctantly he said O.K.

I was with Al over a period of four or five months. On Saturday and Sunday nights, after our four or five shows a day at the Brooklyn Paramount, we doubled out at the Pavillon Royal on the Merrick Road in Valley Stream, Long Island. The same people I'd worked for at the Roman Pools Casino, Christo and Steinberg —Steinberg is now the manager of the Hillcrest Country Club in Los Angeles, California—ran the Pavillon Royal.

The Pavillon Royal seated about eight hundred people. It was a beautiful place, set in a garden, and built by Paul and Sam Salvin and James Thompson especially for entertainment purposes. The Pavillon Royal was their country night club. They controlled nine night clubs in New York. Paul Salvin and Jimmy Thompson were the most important night club impresarios in America in the early twenties. They owned the Little Club, the Palais Royal, and the Montmartre, which was very exclusive and strictly black tie. And they had the Plantation, which featured Negro shows and a four-dollar cover charge. Ethel Waters and Florence Mills started there and the famous song, "Dinah," was introduced at the Plantation. Lew Leslie produced those shows, and the four-dollar cover didn't bother anyone in those days. It was so hard to get in you were happy to be admitted at any price.

These boys had another club called the Moulin Rouge, which offered girl shows and catered to a different clientele, the out-of-town buyers. And at the Little Club they had stars like Marian Harris and Bee Palmer, all very individual singers.

I went over pretty good at the Pavillon Royal. There was a lot of talk; about me, all of it favorable. Word got around: "There's a girl singer out at the Pavillon Royal who has that thing."

It was Steinberg who originated a form of entertainment he called Sunday Night Impromptu Entertainment—he'd started it many years before, in 1913, with Sophie Tucker, at Reisenweber's Café—and it reached its peak at the Pavillon Royal. A lot of performers came out there on Saturday or Sunday night because they liked the food, but mostly because it was a good, flashy showcase in which to break in an act, and sometimes Steinberg called upon them.

But to take care of not having impromptu entertainment on hand to do a whole show, he always had some of the agents he knew bring a reserve supply of paid entertainment out. An M.C.

75

would say, "I'd like to introduce So-and-so," and somebody like Jay C. Flippen would come on; fellows like that.

On Steinberg's fiftieth birthday a few years ago, sixteen kids came over to his place one Sunday. Among them were Judy Garland, Jackie Cooper, Deanna Durbin, Mickey Rooney, Peggy Ryan, and Freddie Bartholomew. As a result of Steinberg's impromptu entertainment system, they'd all gotten themselves jobs at Metro-Goldwyn-Mayer.

Well, one Sunday night back at the Pavillon Royal one of Steinberg's sources of supply was Lou Irwin. Lou brought me out to the Pavillon Royal. I was wearing a simple little dress and I sang "Singing in the Rain." Steinberg was in the kitchen, so he didn't hear me, but when he came out to join his friends and his wife at his table, he heard a terrific blast of applause, and his wife said, "That little girl is good." So Steinberg came over and asked me my name. When I told him he asked, "Do you know another song?"

I said, "Yes, sir."

He suggested that I sing it, and once more I got a hand from the crowd. Steinberg listened; then he told Lou Irwin, "Bring her out here again next Sunday."

Our engagement of one week at the Brooklyn Paramount spread out to seven weeks that spring, and before long Steinberg was asking me to come out to the Pavillon Royal two nights a week: Saturday and Sunday. Sunday was the important one. The place was jammed then. It was quite a thing for a girl to sing with a name band like Guy Lombardo's behind her.

The word about the girl at the Pavillon Royal who had that

thing filtered up and down Broadway, and one day Vinton Freedley, a Broadway producer with a big reputation, caught my act at the Brooklyn Paramount.

Alex Aarons and Vinton Freedley were producing and casting a show called *Girl Crazy*. It had music and lyrics by George and Ira Gershwin, a book by Guy Bolton and Jack McGowan, and starred Ginger Rogers. Originally this show was written for Bert Lahr, but Bert had signed with George White for a show called *Flying High,* and he wasn't available. After a lot of discussion it was decided to sign Willie Howard to play the Lahr part in *Girl Crazy*. Ginger Rogers' leading man was Allen Kearns. I was put in to sing three songs, one called "I Got Rhythm," another called "Sam and Delilah," and the third was "Boy! What Love Has Done to Me."

Freedley had signed Ginger at the then fantastic salary of fifteen hundred dollars a week. She had created a furor in the movie *Young Man of Manhattan*. She was pretty, she could act, she could dance, but no one called her The Voice. Ginger's voice was a pleasing one, but small. The way she sang "Embraceable You" was charming, but the songs she sang didn't require power.

Girl Crazy had Willie Howard as its comedian; he couldn't sing much. And it had Allen Kearns as its juvenile; he wasn't Pinza. For its specialty dance it had the DeMarcos, Tony and Renée. They weren't supposed to sing, even if they could. And with a Gershwin score you had to have somebody who could sing. Luckily for me, even then I had a powerful delivery. I was using much the same technique and doing much the same things with my voice that I do now.

77

Vinton Freedley came over to the Brooklyn Paramount and caught me there. When I came off stage, he introduced himself. I didn't know him from Adam to look at, but his name meant something to me all right. I was smart enough to know that Vinton Freedley was a producer; and he said he wanted to sign me for his show.

After Freedley caught me in Brooklyn, he arranged for me to meet George Gershwin, so George could hear me sing and I could hear the score he'd written. I was told to come to Gershwin's apartment at 33 Riverside Drive, between shows at the Brooklyn Paramount, so I still had my make-up on when I got there. Ira Gershwin was there, too, and George played the songs he'd written for the show, especially those I was to sing if I got the job.

Then I sang two or three of the swing numbers I'd been doing in night clubs and vaudeville. Freedley says the tunes I sang for Gershwin in his penthouse on Riverside Drive were "Little White Lies" and "Exactly Like You," but I was so excited at the whole deal that, for all I remember, I might have sung "London Bridge Is Falling Down."

It was the first time I'd met George Gershwin, and if I may say so without seeming sacrilegious, to me it was like meeting God. Imagine the great Gershwin sitting down and playing his songs for Ethel Agnes Zimmermann, of Astoria, Long Island. No wonder I was tongue-tied.

When he played "I Got Rhythm," he told me, "If there's anything about this you don't like, I'll be happy to change it." There was nothing about that song I didn't like. But that's the kind of guy he was. I'll never forget it.

I smiled and nodded, but I didn't say anything. I was too busy thinking how to phrase the music. Gershwin seemed puzzled at my silence. Finally he said again, "If there's anything about these songs you don't like, Miss Merman, I'll be happy to make changes."

It wasn't that; it was only that I was so flabbergasted. Through the fog that had wrapped itself around me, I heard myself say, "They will do very nicely, Mr. Gershwin."

There were those who thought my reply funny when it was repeated to them, as if I'd given the great Gershwin the old hauteur treatment. I was so drunk with the glory of it all that I could have said anything, but whatever I said, I meant it to be grateful and humble. That's for sure.

At the end of the session, I was signed for *Girl Crazy* at $375 per week. Al Siegel was signed with me. I was given "Sam and Delilah," a torchy, narrative song, and "I Got Rhythm" to do, and a couple of lines to cue me into my songs. When we went into rehearsal and it was discovered that I could read lines pretty well, I was given a few more.

Buck Crouse and Howard Lindsay, those two cutup playwright pals of mine, think they're very funny when they say, "There was terrific excitement in the Zimmermann home when they discovered that Ethel could talk *too*."

They don't really mean that as bluntly as they put it. It's just their way. What they mean to say is I'd only been singing up to that point. I was only supposed to sing songs in *Girl Crazy*, and utter just enough lines to cue me into those songs; then all of a sudden I was given lines to say, although not many of them. I'd never had the chance to read lines before, but after that a small part was written in for me. It wasn't that I deliberately gave the first few lines they handed me a comic effect; I read them as naturally as I knew how, but my reading of them seemed to send people off into howls of laughter. According to Crouse and Lindsay, who are great ones for wringing every last drop of juice from a story, my mom and pop went around telling the neighbors proudly, "Ethel can talk."

In the meantime, Irwin had booked Siegel and me into the Palace Theater in New York. The jump from the Brooklyn Paramount to the Palace Theater was a tall one. Every variety artist's ambition was to play the Palace, but they usually had to play the entire country before they got there. Some of them played a whole career in show business and never played the Palace at all. I played it as my second big engagement.

I finished my second show at the Palace and snagged a taxi up to the Alvin Theater to rehearse for *Girl Crazy*. I rehearsed for *Girl Crazy* in the morning at the Alvin, drove back to the Palace to do a matinee, came back to the Alvin to rehearse, went back to the Palace to do a night show, and came back to rehearse once more. It was a grind. I didn't get much sleep.

In *Girl Crazy* I played Kate Fothergill, the wife of a guy who ran the gambling room at a dude ranch. Billy Kent played my husband. Ginger Rogers played the part of Molly, the postmistress of Custerville, Arizona, where the action took place.

Vinton didn't know whether I'd collapse with stage fright when I first sang in the big league or not, but he was taking no chance. He made me lean against the proscenium arch. I wore a black skirt slashed up to there, and a red waist cut low in front. Thus clad—or unclad—I leaned against that arch on the stage and sang "Sam and Delilah."

During the rehearsals in Philadelphia, Al Siegel was taken sick and when the show came to New York he went into a hospital. He came out of the hospital and played the show opening night in New York, but after that his health didn't let him continue. We had to get another pianist quickly. So we approached Roger Edens, the pianist with Red Nichols' band, who was playing in the pit. Roger was scared to death, because he'd never been on a stage in his life, but he finally consented to go on if the spotlights were kept off him and he could be hidden in protective darkness. Today Roger is a top musical producer and composer at M-G-M; he produced the recent Metro hit musical, *Deep in My Heart*, and he coached Judy Garland during her Metro career.

Gershwin openings were important on Broadway. The opening night of *Girl Crazy* in New York was no exception. In show biz, it's what you do in New York that counts. You may have done all right elsewhere, but you haven't really done it until you face a New York first-night crowd. That's when the chips are down.

It's very hard for me to stand back and take a cold, calm look at that first night of *Girl Crazy*. It's still thunder in the back of my head. I didn't know what was happening to me. When I did my first number, opened my mouth, and let out: " 'Delilah was a floozy,' " everybody screamed and yelled, and there was so much noise that I thought something had fallen out of the loft onto the stage. That was only the beginning.

As I went into the second chorus of "I Got Rhythm," I held a note for sixteen bars while the orchestra played the melodic line —a big, tooty thing—against the note I was holding. By the time I'd held that note for four bars the audience was applauding. They applauded through the whole chorus and I did several encores.

It seemed to do something to them. Not because it was sweet or beautiful, but because it was exciting.

Few dames have the ability to project a big note and hold it. It's not just a matter of breath; it's a matter of power in the diaphragm. I'd never trained my diaphragm, but I must have had a strong one. When I finished that song I still didn't get the meaning of what happened. I knew people were beating their hands together and I had to sing encore after encore, but all the noise and excitement made me sluggy.

I've heard honest—and even intelligent—people describe that first time they heard "I Got Rhythm" as a "high point in the theater." It was the kind of thing that happened when Mary Martin sang "My Heart Belongs to Daddy."

During the intermission George Gershwin came up to me and said, "Ethel, do you realize what's happened to you?"

"No," I told him.

All I knew was I'd gone out and had sung "I Got Rhythm" the

way I'd been told to sing it; the audience had seemed to think me a new type singer, and they'd liked it.

George gave me a funny look and told me, "Don't ever let anybody give you a singing lesson. It'll ruin you."

Chapter Six

The day after the opening of *Girl Crazy* I had a lunch date with George, who asked me, "Have you seen the notices in the papers?"

"No," I said. "To be real truthful with you, George, I haven't had the time."

He looked at me as if I were nuts or something, then pulled a batch of *Girl Crazy* notices from his pocket and showed them to me. I read them, but I couldn't believe them. I just sat there with my mouth open. My name was scattered through those clippings, but it was like reading about somebody else. It sounded as if the reviewers had written their stuff sacked in on a bunk in an opium den.

"Get them!" I kept saying. "Get them! What are they, hop-heads or something?"

Some of the comments made about that show meant so much

to me that I saved them up and I offer them here with pardonable pride: "*Girl Crazy*'s chief claim to fame lies in the fact that it was the cradle for the birth of another blues singer, Ethel Merman. Her trim little body was dragged up by the hair from a night club to the boards of the Alvin. . . . Her baby stare belies knowing anatomical curves. . . . Ethel isn't mournful, like Libby Holman. She isn't tear-stained and voice-cracked, like Helen Morgan. . . . She approaches sex in song with the cold fury of a philosopher. She aims at a point slightly above the entrails, but she knocks you out just the same."

How about that? I ask you! That guy could really write, couldn't he? As I recall it, he was some anonymous genius on *Time* magazine. I don't know how he could write so good up against a weekly deadline.

I knew that I'd stopped that *Girl Crazy* show—people had kept dinning that at me—but I hadn't known I was *that* good.

For those who've heard the phrase "stopping the show," and wonder what it means, this is it; I found out in *Girl Crazy*. It means that the show can't go on because the audience insists on having a song or a dance done over and over until they've had their fill of it. This can take a long time.

You know you've got a show stopper on your hands when the applause for a principal who's just done his stuff refuses to die down when another principal walks on stage. So the principal who's walked out into the storm of applause goes back to his dressing room and broods about throat-cutting. It doesn't matter much whose throat.

If a producer or director is farsighted enough to see that a certain thing is going to be a show stopper, he'll send out a couple of chorus girls to ask, "Have you seen Jimmy lately?" or something equally unimportant. That way there'll be an interval before another important member of the cast comes on. So much for "show stopping."

I could get off a lot of stuff about how "I meditate my roles," but it would be hooey. "Meditate" is for Theatre Guild performers. When I get a part I study it; then I do it. I go to rehearsals and listen to direction. I make sure I know what I'm doing on opening night, and that I know the lyrics and the book backward and forward.

But this doesn't explain how I get laughs or why I've been successful as a comedienne. Part of this is due to the fact that the people who've written my lines—people like Dorothy Fields or Howard Lindsay or Buck Crouse—know what I can deliver and what I can't deliver. But *why* I can deliver a certain type thing I don't know. Could be the wide-eyed, startled look I was born with or the duck-legged way I walk, but mostly I guess it's instinctive timing and just being natural.

I do know it's not in planning it, not in deliberately trying to make it funny, not in saying, "Here comes a funny line, folks." The idea is to hit them with a loaded line while they're unaware.

Many times I've been asked, "Do you have to know exactly what the lyric writer means by his words?"

This is a silly question. The answer is obvious. I wouldn't know how the gargle-and-steam-radiator school of singing feels about it, but I can't sing anything I don't understand. In *Annie Get Your Gun,* every time I sang "Moonshine Lullaby" there were tears in my eyes. It was that touching. I couldn't have got teary about it unless I was thinking the words as well as singing them, could I? I never got bored with that song. It's one of my favorites. They couldn't play it on the radio, so it didn't become popular. It was ruled off the air because it contained a reference to liquor. There was a thing in it about Pappy working in the moonlight behind a hill at a busy little still.

But even if I don't know how I get the effects I get, I have enough sense to know that I do all right. I'd be a dope if I didn't know that, and I'd be even dopier if I changed the way I do it. A singing teacher tells you when and where to breathe. I breathe when I want to. I was afraid that if I ever took a lesson the professor would try to change my breathing, and I'd take a breath even if I didn't have to take one because the rules said it was time to take it. Each time I was tempted to sign on with some voice professor, I thought of George Gershwin telling me never to do it and that stopped me.

Nor do I do anything to save my voice. Somebody once told me that Lily Pons uses honey to keep her pipes lubricated and sweet. I just stand up and holler and hope that my voice holds out. So far, it's always been there when I needed it.

While I'm on the subject of my personal beliefs, I don't hold with exercise. My idea is that it's unhealthy. The way I see it, even having yourself massaged is bad for you. It's liable to soften your muscles. I feel all right without it, so why start it and get used to it?

You might call my feeling about that an oddity. Well, if that's odd, how about this: creamed tripe is one of my favorite dishes.

Eleanor Holm is a long-standing pal of mine. Sometimes when I had a matinee and a night show, too, I didn't go home between shows—and Eleanor would rush a growler of creamed tripe into my dressing room. It's like chicken à la king, except it's based on tripe instead of chicken. It's not a big piece of tripe with cream on top. It's chopped up into squares and put into a cream sauce. I haven't eaten creamed tripe in a long time. I don't seem to see it around much any more. When I ask for creamed tripe, the waiters shy away and turn pale.

But if my passion for creamed tripe seems different from other people's yens, I'm real normal in a way you wouldn't expect. People always expect theatrical folk to sleep until twelve or one o'clock every day. I've never done that. I get up early and go shopping. Many times at a quarter past nine in the morning I'm standing in front of a store waiting to get in. It's different when I stay out late. Then I have to get my rest like anybody else, but if I'm home at a reasonable hour I'm up with the birds—that is, if the birds are inclined to be light sleepers.

But to get back to that lunch date I had with George Gershwin. He told me that he was glad to have somebody sing his songs the way he'd written them. Composers don't like people taking liberties with their stuff. If you don't watch some singers, they'll trick up a melody with falsettos and all like that. Cole Porter is very strict about it. Dick Rodgers is too. Dick likes his songs introduced very simply in a show. If someone wants to trick them up later, that's O.K. After a song has become a hit, a composer may say, "Let Susie Slugg slug it around until it's unrecognizable." He doesn't say that when she's introducing it.

88

Fewer and fewer songs are sung the way they're written any more. This kind of thing is not for me. My motto is: "Leave them the way they came out of the composer's head." If it's a good head, they'll be good songs without my editing them.

Sometimes you don't recognize a song when you hear it on radio or TV, although you were very fond of it when you heard it the first time. That means it's been overarranged to death. In the Decca recording studios on Fifty-seventh Street in New York there hangs a sign. It asks: WHERE'S THE MELODY? This sign is there because Decca wants to sell records. The people who head that company are not stupid.

Girl Crazy ran for forty weeks. For those days that was good. But it could have folded—at least temporarily—if I'd made a slight miscalculation in swallowing. I love to chew gum. It's one of my favorite pastimes. Many's the time I've forgotten to rid myself of my gum before rushing on stage, and I've found myself playing a whole scene with it parked in my cheek.

I could handle a pretty good-size slug of peanut brittle the same way. Willie Howard, the comedian whose hair looked like a fright wig and whose nose looked like a gimlet, used to hand me large chunks of peanut brittle and bet me that I couldn't eat it while I was singing. I rose to that challenge like a sportswoman. I'd go on singing "I Got Rhythm" and holding a note for sixteen bars, with a large consignment of brittle tucked away in the side of my mouth.

I haven't tried it for a long time and I don't think I could do it now. If that stuff had ever got stuck in my throat, they would have to drop the curtain and fish for it. I might even be an oxygen pump job.

While I'm at it, you may be interested in the difference between the way a big musical show was kicked off then and the way it's promoted today. To a man like Freedley, the whole present system of holding auditions for backers and selling pieces of a show practically at auction is so embarrassing he can't go through with it. For the most part, when it came to getting up the scratch for a show, Vinton used his own money. He set aside part of the take from his last successful show and used it on his next one. He never let more than three or four outsiders help him bank-roll. Two he did let in were Otto Kahn and New York City's mayor, Jimmy Walker.

Jimmy used to get up his share in cash. Halfway through rehearsals, an envelope would arrive at the theater with "Office of the Mayor, City Hall," printed on it. When Vinton opened the envelope, it would be stuffed with thousand-dollar bills. Once the bills fell out and drifted up and down the aisle like leaves blowing around a yard and Vinton had to grub around under the seats, spearing G-notes.

Speaking of Jimmy Walker cues me into the story of the Central Park Casino. It was one of Jimmy's favorite hangouts. After the opening night of *Girl Crazy,* I went to a party in the Casino. I'd been there a few nights before and nobody had noticed me. When I walked in that opening night, people stared at me and whispered and I knew I was in. I *really* knew I was in when the Casino's management asked me to come there and work every night after the *Girl Crazy* curtain.

A lot of people believe that the Central Park Casino was the finest restaurant-night club the world has ever known. There's never been anything like it. Perhaps El Morocco, in New York, and perhaps the Ambassador, in London, are in the same class. I wouldn't know. At El Morocco you see a great many people who used to go to the Central Park Casino, only they're a little older now and they don't dance as fast. You'd walk into the Central Park Casino at night for dinner or for supper any night and you'd see the great and near great from every walk of life. Not only was Jimmy Walker there practically every night, but so were Flo Ziegfeld, Sam Harris, Charles Dillingham, Lee Shubert, and such stars as Noel Coward and Gertrude Lawrence. The song writers Cole Porter, Irving Berlin, the Gershwins, Dick Rodgers, and Larry Hart were patrons too. After the opening of a show it was *the* place.

It's a crime that the Central Park Casino was ever torn down. It was started by important Wall Street and theatrical men and I was told that different brokerage firms also put up pieces of change, contributing ten to fifteen thousand dollars each. It was all engineered by a man named Sidney Solomon, who asked Jimmy Walker to do him a favor and let him open a beautiful night club in Central Park.

Solomon engaged Joseph Urban, who in the opinion of many was the greatest interior decorator and creator of novel color schemes and designs, and Urban built a building around three principal rooms. There was a big room where people danced and dined, and two other rooms for private parties built with a terrace outside.

The filthy rich went there when they wanted to look at each other in their white ties and tails. You had to be in evening dress to get into the dining room. If you weren't, you were shunted into the cocktail room, no matter how much money you had. This wasn't just night club café society. This was Park Avenue society as well.

The Casino was run beautifully. It was the only place in America with only one show a night. All the rest had two or even three. There were always fresh flowers on the tables and there was no nonsense, or fights, or anybody getting too gassed and objectionable.

I'd started in *Girl Crazy* at $375 a week, eight performances a week. Then Freedley raised me to $600. But at the Casino I did one show a night—it lasted twenty to twenty-five minutes—and I was paid $1250 a week for it. As for the bite the income tax put on me in 1930, we should have it so good now!

The crowd on hand for my Casino opening had class. Among those present were Lady Furness, the Earl of Warwick, Leslie Howard, and Ethel Barrymore. After I was done they shook my hand.

My first number was a medley of hits. Then there was a hot piano break and I went into "Delilah was a floozy." A hot piano break is the spot where you don't sing and the piano takes over solo for a few bars. There were more hot works from the band and I finished with the fast, rah-rah-rah-type song, "I Got Rhythm." I've always finished with that. It's my signature.

I had my own special arrangements at the Casino. I'd asked Roger Edens, who was playing piano for me in the pit in *Girl*

92

Crazy, to make them. After that it seemed only natural to bring him to the Casino to play for me there too.

I loved that Central Park Casino. Maybe it's because I've got a wide streak of naïveté in me. When Roger Edens and I went there each night after the theater, we'd stay in one of the back rooms and peer out through the curtains to see what celebrities had showed that particular P.M. Would it be Gertrude Lawrence, or Jimmy Walker, or Lindbergh?

Roger says I didn't seem to realize that I was a star too. He says I was so impressed when Gertie Lawrence was out front that I was gaga. I guess I was still stage-struck, and seeing stars like Lawrence gave me a thrill. All I know is that I got more kick out of those people sitting ringside than I did out of doing the show. Imagine me getting paid to see *them!*

Of course I had to get out and sing a few songs, but that was no trouble. I did that in my shower at home for my own amusement.

My first engagement at the Casino was for thirty weeks. After that I played there on and off until it closed. Behind me was Leo Reisman's orchestra, in which Eddy Duchin's piano playing was one of the big attractions. His touch was a special thing—muted, smooth, wonderful. And he was so good-looking the girls stood around watching him, listening dreamy-pussed, not bothering to dance, just making little rhythmic movements back and forth. Then, when Reisman left, Eddy formed his own band and took over.

After I opened in *Girl Crazy*, Warners wanted to sign me back again at $1500 a week but I wasn't interested. I guess the human

93

thing would have been a big gush of "See? I told you so. You weren't so smart." But between the Casino in the Park and the show at the Alvin, I was too busy to have time for gloating.

After *Girl Crazy* closed, I was booked into the New York Paramount. By this time I'd decided to use two pianists, so I engaged another one to work with Roger Edens. My second pianist was Johnny Green, who is now head of M-G-M's musical organization in Hollywood, and who's one of the real great men in the music business. Among other things, he has written such hits as "Body and Soul," so I was lucky as all get out in the music department.

In those days the theatrical season ended in June and shows shuttered for the summer. So *Girl Crazy* didn't go on the road. In the fall I signed to be in the next of George White's series of *Scandals,* for which the song-writing team of Lew Brown, Buddy De Sylva, and Ray Henderson had written the score.

But before that, when *Girl Crazy* closed, I'd gone up to Lake George with Mom and Pop for a vacation. At the time I had a Chrysler car, special model, one of those long purry jobs, and a chauffeur. We got there on a Saturday night and I told the chauffeur we wanted to go for a drive at eight o'clock Sunday morning. When we came back and went to the desk, they said George White had put in several calls for me.

I called him back. He wanted me to come down on Monday morning to begin working for him, so I took off with Mom and Pop. I sent the chauffeur back to get the trunks and bring them to Long Island.

The show had opened in Atlantic City and opening night everyone knew that it was in trouble. Lew Brown had written ten successful *George White's Scandals,* and he had tossed off as many consecutive hits as any Broadway writer in the business. He was not only a great lyric writer but a fine comedy writer as well. I saw the show with my agent, Lou Irwin, and we didn't think the songs such a much. Also, there was a shortage of personalities. So Irwin was asked to make a deal for me. It was agreed that new songs would be put in and I joined the cast.

Since then, Cole Porter has told me that he's always been fascinated by the song "Life Is Just a Bowl of Cherries" in this show. The rhyme, "Don't take it serious, it's too mysterious," haunts him. He says that rhyming "serious" with "mysterious" "staggers the human mind." Whether it made the human mind stagger or just weave and bob is neither here nor there since Mr. White's extravaganza ran seven months. I call that good staggering.

George White was a nice man to work for, but I never really got to know him. I just knew him as a boss, the way I'd known my boss Caleb Bragg. After the *Scandals,* I went for more vaudeville. That was in 1932. I was booked into the Palace on a summer bill. Billy Gaxton, Lou Holtz, and I were the headliners. When I had to leave to rehearse for a new stage musical, Kate Smith took my place.

A producer, Larry Schwab, had asked me to be in a musical called *Humpty Dumpty.* He had hired Dick Whiting, Nacio Herb Brown, and Buddy De Sylva to write the songs and all hands were trying for "a different approach to musical comedy." The idea was to string together a series of sketches that would kid the pants off of American history. But "different approach" or

95

not, the boys didn't have the right songs for me. Although that song-writing team was great when they were with it, the ones they'd fluffed up for *Humpty Dumpty* were for two other girls.

When I mentioned, in my shy and shrinking way, that they hadn't come up with any really great songs for me, a trouble-shooting conference was held. During the course of the conversation they asked my accompanist and arranger, Roger Edens, if he had any ideas.

"Buddy De Sylva had an idea for a number I liked," Roger said. "All three of you had a tune for it, but it's been shelved. It was called 'Eadie Was a Lady.' Remember? It's all about Eadie having class with a capital K."

Eadie had been shelved because it was clear that she had been what my grandmother called a "soiled dove," and Larry Schwab wanted to keep his show on a high satirical plane. But Roger Edens kept saying, "This material is automatically wonderful for Merman." In the end they told him, "If you think it's so wonderful and you think you can do something with it, go ahead, work on it."

Roger worked all night. By morning he had developed a sketch that was and still is one of the greatest. Since then, Eadie, the girl with Klass, the dame who stuck her little finger out when she drank brandy, has become a part of our national song life, along with a frail named Frankie, who had a man who "done her wrong," and a doll named Jenny, who "would make up her mind," and Minnie, who "had a heart as big as a whale."

The sketch began with patter about what Eadie could do and

what she couldn't do. It was sung by a broad—who was never going to be mistaken for the headmistress of a seminary—to the blondes who were flouncing around the house after Eadie's funeral, remembering how ladylike Eadie had been. I was the brassy biddy who sang the song.

It all added up to a musical saga in honor of Eadie's gentility. Eadie had nothing to do with the *Humpty Dumpty* story line (whatever that was); it was a production number within the show. A bunch of sailors were sitting around mourning with the girls when I made my entrance down a stairway in a satin dress that was the deep rich red color of American Beauty roses. My hair was done in a pompadour and I had a black boa around my neck. I was swinging my hips; my skirt was slit in front and I was tickling the sailors under the chin. In short, I was a dish. As I finished each verse of my lament for Eadie, the sailors and the girls chimed in with a touching choral.

Roger added some lyrics of his own and played the whole thing for me, and I liked it a lot. Then he played it for Buddy De Sylva, and Buddy liked it too. But as I recall it, Larry Schwab still said he didn't think it was in a class with the rest of the material.

"It's in a class with me," I said. "And I want to do it."

Things were getting tough; we had only two weeks left before opening, and the others said, "Let's let Roger go ahead with it." Larry went along too. The scenic designer built a sporty little room in which the girls could sit and mourn. The costume designer designed costumes that were a combination of funeral decorum and the mad, bad life.

Then, zongo! *Humpty Dumpty* opened in Pittsburgh and not to put too fine a point upon it, it stunk up the joint. In Junior League words, it was a fiasco.

Nothing went over except "Eadie." The arty sketches were nothing. All those little satirical vignettes of American history lay there while "Eadie" went to glory. The next day one Pittsburgh paper didn't even call the show *Humpty Dumpty*. Its reviewer said, *"Eadie Was a Lady opened last night."*

It was decided to close the show and begin all over again. Plenty of rewriting was done, and when we hit the road for another tryout, the show's leading comedian was Jack Haley. The way I remember it, two of the songs salvaged were "Eadie" and another song, "You're an Old Smoothie," which some of the Betty Co-eds and Joe Colleges of that day will remember. Vincent Youmans was imported to pump in some new songs, and the production was retitled *Take a Chance*.

Sometimes rewriting, tinkering, and revamping doesn't work, but *Take a Chance* was a hit. The biggest thrill Roger Edens has ever had was when the New York *Times* printed the lyrics of "Eadie"—in full—the week of the New York opening. The New York *Times* yet! Roger almost burst with pride. On the strength of this, he was given a chance to go to Hollywood, where he later worked on *Kid Millions*, a movie I made with Eddie Cantor for Sam Goldwyn.

When *Take a Chance* finished its New York run, it was taken to Chicago. I went with it. But there just wasn't the excitement there was in being in a show in New York in wintertime. There was none of that crispness in the air that goes with football or a

Broadway fall opening. A fall night in New York, with the fur coats shining under the marquee lights and the gentlemen in black ties and Chesterfields, made my insides tingle as well as my skin.

Chapter Seven

My next was *Anything Goes*. In it was my personal nomination for the finest comedy team who ever worked, Billy Gaxton and Victor Moore.

The story of how *Anything Goes* reached the boards was as crazy as any of the stories the musical shows of those days were built around—and they were built around some real crazy stuff. Vinton Freedley's associate, Alex Aarons, was eaten up by the idea that it would be wonderful to have the British matinee idol and song-and-dance man, Jack Buchanan, in a show for him.

Vinton thought it would be fine, too, *if* the show could be an intimate-review-type thing built around Buchanan, since Buchanan had scored a resounding success in such productions; otherwise not. But "otherwise" was the kind of show Aarons had in mind, so Vinton took a powder.

"You do this one on your own," he said. "I'll sit it out."

In addition to Buchanan, whom he'd hired at three thousand dollars a week, Aarons had Jack Pearl, who was then at the height of his Baron Munchausen radio fame, and Lyda Roberti. He'd also signed Morrie Ryskind, who had written the book for *Of Thee I Sing*, and he'd lined up Herbie Fields, George Gershwin, and Ira Gershwin. Aarons did things in a big way, only in this case he was doing them with small money. He was financially committed up to his eyeballs, but the nickels in his pants were scarce.

As Vinton tells it, one morning Alex came to him looking pea-green, and said, "I'm in a jam. I've made an eight-week guarantee for Buchanan. That's twenty-four thousand. And I've made a six-week guarantee for Roberti. That's six thousand more. And I have no do-re-mi."

"I'll take over," Vinton told him. "You go lie down somewhere. You need it."

The show was called *Pardon My English*. It was a moot question—whatever moot means—whether Vinton was taking over the show or the show was taking over Vinton. It cost ninety thousand dollars, which was very heavy sugar for those days. *Pardon My English* ran for ten weeks at the Majestic Theater—and lost five thousand dollars a week. Then Vinton's creditors closed in on him, waving their arms menacingly, and Vinton closed the show. He told his wife, "We'll go some place and hide until I can catch up." He took her to Panama on a fruit boat, en route to Tobago, an island north of Trinidad. Then they holed up there and he quit panting. They spent four or five months while Vinton put splints on his bank loan and bandaged it. When he'd paid off his creditors he came home.

While on Tobago he hired a little boat, did some fishing, and tried to think of a story around which to build his next show. He had Billy Gaxton and Victor Moore in mind for his comeback production and he wanted me again. He hoped to do a thing with music by Cole Porter. Vinton had always worked with George Gershwin but Gershwin had gone operatic. He wasn't interested in writing a straight musical-show score at the moment.

Having been a guy on a boat himself for a while, Vinton naturally thought of a story about a guy on a boat—or rather, two guys and a gal on a boat. He came back from Tobago, got hold of me, and outlined the story he had in mind. It sounded fine.

I notice that nowadays in the theater they don't seem to need the comics they used to need. There was a time when the producer of a big Broadway musical wouldn't think of doing a show without first having a Bert Lahr, a Victor Moore, a Willie or Eugene Howard, a Jimmy Durante, or a Bobby Clark lined up. Now they don't think along those lines. To me, that's both Broadway's and the public's loss.

The shows have changed too. Now they're based on a story that's already been written. I don't know how closely *Guys and Dolls* followed the Runyon stories, but *Pajama Game* was skimmed off the top of the book, *7½ Cents*; *Wonderful Town* from *My Sister Eileen*; *Carousel* from *Liliom*; *Oklahoma!* from *Green Grow the Lilacs*; and *South Pacific* from the Michener *Tales* of the same name.

The writers who used to think up the books that were wrapped around Gershwin and Cole Porter scores started from scratch, with only their bare cupboards and an unmanageable sense of humor to guide them. First a producer signed a cast; then he hired writers to rustle up some material for that cast to use. "I've got Bert Lahr," he'd say; "write me a part for Bert Lahr." Or, "I've signed Victor Moore. Get goin', buddy. Make with the Moore-type yuks."

Assembling the various ingredients of *Anything Goes* was quite a problem. When Vinton finally got in touch with Cole Porter, he found him floating down the Rhine in a boat. Freedley wanted Guy Bolton and P. G. Wodehouse as his writers, but Bolton—who had written *Sally*; and *Rosalie* and *Lady Be Good* with collaborators—was in England, and Bolton's writing partner, Wodehouse, was rusticating in France. To line these two up, Vinton boarded the *Majestic* and headed for Europe. He scooped up Bolton and took him to Le Touquet in France, where Wodehouse was living. Having got them together, Vinton sketched out the story he had in mind. According to Vinton, they said they thought it was a fine springboard, and that they'd collaborate on it by cross-Channel telephone and mail their script to the U.S.A.

The script finally arrived on August fifteenth. It was called *Hard to Get*. Vinton had hired Howard Lindsay to direct the show and he turned the script over to him. It was laid on a ship all right—but a ship that sank. Vinton's reaction to that was an anguished: "This is funny?"

A few days later the S.S. *Morro Castle* burned off Asbury Park in New Jersey with a loss of 134 lives. That did it. If there ever had been anything funny about a sinking ship there was nothing funny about it now.

In the understatement of the year Vinton told Lindsay, "We're in trouble." Howard agreed.

"You're going to have to revise it," Vinton said.

Howard didn't agree. "I won't be able to bang a typewriter twelve hours a day and direct this show too," he said. "You'll have to get somebody in to help."

Vinton asked Cole Porter if he knew of a good playwright's assistant who was running around loose. Cole said, "No." But that night Cole ran into his old friend, the magazine-cover artist, Neysa McMein, at a party. At eight o'clock the next morning Neysa called Cole.

"I dreamed about a man for you," she said. "Russel Crouse."

"What is a Russel Crouse?" Cole asked. Cryptic, that Porter, especially when roused at eight in the morning.

"This Russel Crouse is a press agent for the Theatre Guild," Neysa said.

"Has he ever written anything?" Cole asked.

"Just press releases," Neysa said.

It didn't seem promising, but in the past some of Neysa's dreams had paid off so Cole called Vinton.

"Where do I find this Crouse?" Vinton asked.

"I understand that his window is right across the street from your office," Cole said. "Just wave at him. You've probably been looking at him for ten years."

Vinton called Crouse and said, "Will you come over and meet a fellow called Howard Lindsay?"

"I'd like to meet a fellow named Howard Lindsay," Buck Crouse said.

So that's how the firm of Lindsay and Crouse was born. If it hadn't been for Neysa's dream, there would have been no *Life with Father*, no *State of the Union*, no *Call Me Madam*.

That would have been a loss. It wasn't strictly true that Crouse had only done press releases. He had done a musical show that had been a flop. "Perhaps it was one of the greatest flops of all time," he said. It was a show called *The Gang's All Here*. And with Corey Ford he had done a moderately successful show for Joe Cook, called *Hold Your Horses*, but he realized he had a long road before him. He had to study the theater, he had to learn about it; he had to know his business.

Howard and Buck began to revise like mad, but the time was so short that we went into rehearsal with only one small scene in a bar of a ship completed. There was still a ship in the story but this one didn't sink.

When Howard and Buck met me to tell me about my part, they had nothing for me. They didn't even have a character in mind. They had to dream up one. So they came up with this idea of a night club girl who mixed biblical talk with slang because there was a preacher on board the same ship—even if he was only a make-believe reverend. One example was "Out of the mouths of babes and suckers." That line didn't stay in the show. But I did have the line "They say it's better to marry than to burn. Boy, am I hot?" After that one they got the curtain down quickly.

Howard and Buck worked day and night and we finally went into rehearsal because Freedley couldn't postpone the thing any longer; he had opening dates out of town. By the time rehearsals started all we had was the first act—and that had large holes in it. Suddenly we'd come to an empty place in the book and Howard and Buck would say, "Now this is a very funny scene which we haven't written."

At the end of the first day's rehearsal one of the actors, Pacie Ripple, went up to Buck and asked, "When do we get the second act?"

"To tell you the truth, we've got some revisions to make on the second act," Buck said.

The truth is, he didn't even know what was to be in it.

Vinton had to order scenery for the other scenes, so he told Don Oenslager, who was doing the settings, "Give me a sort of interior with an exterior feeling."

Don shook his head groggily, but he was equal to the occasion. He cooked up a scene which would fit anywhere, any place, any time. It had some walls and some lattice and some vines on the walls. There was an arch in front of some steps. You could have called it anything.

When we took off for Boston for the tryout, we still had no last scene down on paper. Vinton mentioned this plaintively to Lindsay and Crouse and they said, "Stop fidgeting, Vinton. We'll have something."

Dress rehearsal night, Crouse and Lindsay emerged from the men's room with a wad of tissue paper in their hands and announced, "We've just written the last sheet." It was no gag. They actually had just written it.

This was one of the greatest feats of revision ever done in a

Broadway musical show because Howard and Russel were only a few lines ahead of us all the way. They wrote on and on late into the night and the next day they'd come in and rehearse what they had written the night before.

The story of *Anything Goes* was a very simple one. Like all musical-comedy stories of the era, plotwise the story was nothing to make Shakespeare twirl in his grave. Billy Gaxton was saying good-by on board ship to the girl he loved. She was going to Europe to marry a title (forced marriage by her parents). Reno Sweeney, a night club singer, was taking her troupe of girls to Europe for personal appearances. She was in love with Gaxton but, of course, he loved the other girl. Victor Moore played Public Enemy No. 13, and he came on the stage in disguise, dressed as a parson, a Rev. Dr. Moon. He carried a fiddle case around with him, but inside there was a submachine gun. While Gaxton was on board, the ship set sail and, since he didn't have a cabin, the Rev. Dr. Moon let him share his. Presently Billy found out that the Rev. Dr. Moon was an impostor and that actually he was a crook named Moon Face Mooney, although he appeared on the passenger list as the Rev. Dr. Moon.

From then on it was up to the plot to take care of itself. Among other things, there was a revival meeting on shipboard, and Billy and Victor gambled for their clothes with two Chinese. The Chinese won.

Amazingly, in spite of all the chaos at dress rehearsal, the show had one of the greatest opening nights ever seen in Boston. Nothing had to be changed for New York. Nothing! Cole Porter had written several extra songs for the show, and we tried one of them out during the out-of-town run on a Saturday matinee. It was called "When I Walk Down the Aisle with You." Billy Gaxton put on a beard, and Bettina Hall, who was the ingenue leading lady, sang it to Billy, but it was taken out after the matinee. We didn't need it. The show was strong enough without it. It had a great Cole Porter score—which means one of the greatest.

When Buck and Howard got to the theater opening night in Boston, they were told that a well-dressed young man had walked up to the box office and had asked to see the company manager, Lou Loewenstein.

The stranger was shown into the manager's office, which was just behind the box office.

He asked, "You the company manager?" and Lou said, "Yes."

"I just wanted to leave a message," the man said. "I'm not concerned personally in this, I'm just giving you this message from the boys in New Jersey. Change the name of Moon Face Mooney. Don't ring up tonight with the name of Moon Face Mooney in the show. If you do, you won't count up the house to figure the size of your bank deposit." Then he walked out.

Loewenstein was pale, Freedley was pale, they were all worried; but when Buck and Crouse heard it, they said, "Nuts. Somebody's kiddin'."

"Wait a minute," Vinton said. "Lou's got a wife. He's got two children. You can't do this to him."

In the end Buck and Howard went backstage into the dressing rooms and told the cast that the character called Moon Face Mooney was to be called Moon Face Martin.

When the curtain went up the first one who had to use the

name was Vera Dunn. When she came out she said, "They don't know you're Moon Face Mooney," then she gasped—realized she'd goofed, and yelled, "I mean MARTIN!" in panic-stricken tones.

Later Buck asked Damon Runyon if he'd ever heard of a mobster named Moon Face Mooney. Damon said, "I'll inquire around and find out."

After a while Damon told Buck, "Your pal was a member of a certain mob from New Jersey. He's a little nuts. He's their patsy and the other members of the mob like to spoof him."

What had happened was that they had heard about Moon Face Mooney being in our show and they had kidded this guy and said, "You're not going to let them do this to you, are you?" And they'd gotten Mr. Mobster Mooney all stirred up to a point where he was sending messages that if his name wasn't changed there'd be trouble.

Also on the opening night in Boston, Billy Gaxton had a love scene on deck with Bettina Hall. Billy had on white tie and tails, and the audience was supposed to think the couple had stayed up there until four or five in the morning, necking. Afterward, Billy was to make an entrance into his stateroom, find Victor Moore, and say, "What a night, what a dawn, what a sunrise!"

The trouble was Billy had forgotten that he was to go into the next scene without changing costume, and in making his quick run from the poop deck he'd absent-mindedly taken off his trousers. After leaving the girl on deck, he entered the stateroom with his trousers draped over his arm, and said, "What a night, what a dawn, what a sunrise!"

I eyed Lindsay and Crouse, who looked as if they wanted to hide under the Plymouth Rock, and I thought, *Well, here we go, closed in Boston the first night.* Somehow it blew over. Maybe the guardians of Boston's morals wrote it off as good clean fun; anyhow, they held their fire.

One line from that show I thought a wow. Victor Moore, Public Enemy No. 13, upheld capital punishment by declaring stoutly, "It was good enough for my father and it's good enough for me." That I liked.

I also liked the word "terrifically" in my song "I Get a Kick Out of You." I took liberties with that word. I paused in the song after the syllable "rif." It was just a way of phrasing, of breaking a word into syllables and holding onto one syllable longer than I ordinarily would, but for some reason that pause killed the people. I'm not enough of a musician to know why, but I know it had that effect.

Funny thing about that song, "I Get a Kick Out of You"; when I first heard it I was doubtful about it. It was a straight and simple thing, with no great heat; and I wasn't sure I could do it, never having done a song like it before. I told myself: *No heat, no rhythm, no sock. It's just a beguine.* But darned if it didn't turn out to be the hit of the show. I did it as a prologue, while Billy Gaxton stood there with a glass of champagne in his hand, listening to me sing it.

I like to think I'm Cole's favorite when it comes to singing his songs. Last summer at a party at his house, he was wonderful to me. He proposed a toast in which he called me his "No. 1, then and always." After dinner I went to the piano and sang every song

110

he'd ever written for me. I looked at him while I sang and his eyes were a little dim.

Some years ago Cole had a fall from a horse and broke both of his legs in about five places. Since then he's had about sixty operations. They've had to break and rebreak his legs, and how he's survived such a long-drawn-out ordeal I don't know. I do know it hasn't affected his talent. He's done some mighty good work in that time, but there were three or four years when you wondered if he'd ever work again.

Cole likes to tell people that I can deliberately flat a note to get a comedy effect. He says he doesn't know whether I know I'm doing it or whether I just do it instinctively. I've got a flash for him. If I do it, I do it deliberately. Take the song "Sam and Delilah"—more particularly, take the words "Delilah was a floozy." I hit a deliberate blue note in it to emphasize the word "floozy" and it *does* get an effect in keeping with the character I'm singing about.

Cole also says that I have an "extraordinary" sense of rhythm. If I *do* have one, it was born in me, like my pipes—either you've got it or you haven't. You can't acquire one or learn it. Some people take lesson after lesson and can't beat out a thing.

Another thing I believe is: you don't have to shag your mouth all over your face to enunciate clearly. I pronounce things carefully when I'm singing, but while I may open up wide to get a note out or to make one clear, I don't let the old lip movements run wild. I try to handle my face as if I'm *talking* to you, only musically.

Following the first night of *Anything Goes*, the New York

Herald Tribune printed a thing I couldn't understand. It went like this: "Miss Merman's part of the song goes along bars, so to say, while the orchestra indulges in contrapuntal ripples and wavers which have nothing to do with the tune, and meanwhile also the rhymes themselves fall on first and middle syllables, in a delightfully tricky sort of syncopation which calls for the most delicately accurate timing on the part of all concerned. The dash and precision with which Miss Merman lands each syllable where it belongs is enchanting."

What I finally figured the man must have meant is this: it was a very tricked-up orchestration and the band was playing against me, but I came out ahead. Period.

As a result of the show *Panama Hattie,* I drew another one of these souped-up reviews a little later. Some guy wrote about "the rotary movement of Merman's forearm with which she swung her songs over the footlights, even when she seemed to be throwing them away." According to this Joe, I must have had a characteristic sidewinding forearm gesture. I don't know what movement he referred to; I use my arms a lot and I do a lot of work with my hands. It could have been anything. Critics are always discovering something significant and arty in things you do naturally. If a girl ain't careful she's apt to wind up in the Ballet Russe.

One night during the run of *Anything Goes* I spotted Toscanini out front. This gave me an idea. I went to my dressing room and sent a telegram to the show's musical director. In it I said I was sorry to have to say it but his direction was terrible. I signed it "Toscanini." I added that I realized it was a roundabout way to get the news to him, but that an usher had volunteered to send the wire and it had seemed a good idea. I asked to have it delivered right away at the theater and I timed it so it was delivered during the intermission.

For the last half of the performance the jazz maestro sweated heavily, glared at his musicians, and kept looking back at Toscanini's seat, to see how he was taking the pit music.

I had taken down Cole's lyrics in shorthand so I could study them. I even took them down over the long-distance telephone when Cole was in New York and we needed a fresh supply of choruses in Boston quick because we were giving out with so many encores. In the same way I jotted down stage directions and bits of business suggested to me. This is just one more reason why I'm high on a secretarial course as a preparation for life.

It's because I've been a secretary that I have a certain amount of poise and can handle situations as they come along. I move with efficiency and do things with precision.

This side of me gives my present agent, George Rosenberg, a kick. Rosy is my agent for motion pictures. He's a tall, slow-talking gent of non-Irish extraction who drawls like a Southerner, and he comes up with some of the funniest expressions. He calls my husband, Bob Six, Jumbo. And he calls me Buckshot or The Bomber. I dig that Jumbo, because Six is six times larger than life; but why Buckshot for me?

Anyhow, I love Rosy. He's wonderful.

I do things that amuse Rosy too. He'd been my agent for some time before it dawned on him that when he dropped in on me and said, "I had a talk with So-and-so about such-and-such a proposition for you and he said thus-and-so," I was making notes of what he told me, and jotting down our conversation in short-hand for future reference.

Once when we'd had a business conference with a number of people, I went over to a typewriter, typed it all up from my notes together with multiple carbons, and handed each person present a copy. "Better read this over," I said. "We don't want any trouble about this later, do we?" Rosy got the biggest bang out of that.

It disconcerts some people when it dawns on them that I'm taking down what they're telling me, and sometimes they clam up. But it's a good idea to get it down, so I won't forget it and, what's more important, the other parties won't forget it either. There are times when they need a memory prod.

Speaking of being a gal on a boat, as I was in *Anything Goes*, reminds me of the period in my life when I was an ace yachts-woman. I used to go up to Larchmont to visit some very good friends of mine, Emil Mosbacher and his wife Gertrude. They had a son, Emil, Jr., who was wonderful at the sailboat-racing thing they do at Larchmont. Two or three years ago he went over to England to race. That's how good he is.

I guess I wasn't much help as a crew, but I was allowed to pull a rope or two and do stuff like lowering the boom and handling things. I probably fouled it up, but I helped in another way.

One Sunday when I was on the Mosbacher boat we came in first, but the committee gave the decision to another entry. You're not supposed to yell in a yacht race, or laugh sneeringly at your opponents, or even give them the bird—it's against the rules, like you're supposed to keep your mouth shut when someone's putting or driving in golf—but I yelled, "Hey!" at those dopey judges across the water. Everybody went "Sh-h-h!" but I kept popping off, "We *were* first! I know we were! Some seventeenth assistant commodore booted one!"

The way people acted, you'd have thought I'd blown up a paper bag and busted it in church. But I was right. They had to reverse their decision next morning when the corrected result came out in the New York *Times* sports section. It didn't mention my name or give me an assist, but I didn't care. It said that the Mosbacher boat won the race. "Sh-h-h-h!" indeed.

Chapter Eight

There's a story that when I went to Hollywood to be in my first movie, *We're Not Dressing,* I found it a big nothing, a clambake. The reason this is hard to down is it's true. The story also goes that I found myself bumper to bumper with hoity-toity movie dames so impressed with their own importance that they looked down their noses at my informal, sassy ways. The slide fastener of this part of the story is off the track. When I went to Hollywood to do my first picture, I met no movie stars off the set. I never went to parties because I didn't know anyone. I didn't get close enough to anybody for them to look down their noses at me. There were some long noses out there, but not that long.

Mom was with me. We'd left Pop back in New York. I lived with her at the Ravenswood, on Rossmore, a building Mae West owns. She lives there too. On Christmas Eve, Mom and I didn't know anybody. We were completely isolated in a social way. We had no place to go, so we just sat there. That time had always meant the Zimmermanns being together and everything that goes with Christmas, like trimming the tree and putting out the presents. We looked at each other and blubbered and thought of Pop back in New York.

I guess we Zimmermanns are all-out sentimentalists. At that point we had a little wire-haired terrier named Scrapsie, and on Scrapsie's birthday, which was February 23, we'd have a birthday cake for him. Since Mom and I couldn't be on hand for it that year, Pop sent us a piece of Scrapsie's cake, packed in a box. We loved old Scrapsie. He was a nuisance, but he was cute.

To bob around in the time department for a moment, I guess I haven't changed much, because a lot later I got sentimental over our armed forces too. Once during the last war I dropped in at the Champagne Room at El Morocco with my then husband, Bob Levitt. I noticed a stirring about and a scurrying here and there and I asked, "What's going on?" I was told that it was a birthday party for Louella Parsons. So I sat down and Vincent Youmans came over to visit with us, and we stayed until they began to turn the lights out. There were about five of us left in the room when in walked Dick Barthelmess' wife Jessica with her son, who was wearing a uniform. He had five or six servicemen with him and he told us that he was leaving the next morning. Somebody said, "Ethel, would you sing a couple of songs for the boys? They're going away in the morning."

That got me. I was sure that they were going on a transport and might never come back. I got up and sang "What Say, Let's Be Buddies." I was crying so hard that my mascara was running and I couldn't see the piano, but I kept saying, "They're going away," like a refrain in a funeral dirge.

When I got home I kept on sobbing, "They're going away. They're sailing tomorrow."

Finally Levitt said, "You're out of your mind. Nobody's leaving in the morning." It was his wartime job to know whether they were or not, so I asked tearfully, "Well, where are they going? They must be going *somewhere*."

"They're probably embarking on a long and dangerous voyage to the nearest Hamburg Heaven at the moment," he said.

I never did find out *where* they were going, or when. But I certainly felt sad about it.

To get back to Hollywood. A few years later, when I went to the Coast to be in the movie *Alexander's Ragtime Band*, things were different. I wasn't being lonely and sitting home and crying. I was leaning over in the opposite direction and having a ball. When I ran into self-important Hollywood stars with nothing behind their self-importance, it made me feel perverse. If they were "too, too refeened," I had to wrestle a yen to snap their garters or dig them in the ribs and say, "You said it, sister!"

Nowadays I guess you might say I've been more or less accepted by Hollywood. I had a wonderful time out there working in my last two pictures, *Call Me Madam* and *There's No Business Like Show Business*. I'm asked to Judy Garland's house now or Van and Evie Johnson's house, or Ann Sothern's house, or Cole Porter's house. It's all in getting to know folks and getting them to know you, just like any place else.

But my early exposure to Hollywood was out of focus. On

Broadway, in spite of the fact that I played a hip-swinging Hannah, it was agreed that I was a wholesome type with a sympathetic quality. Hollywood didn't give me a chance to show that. The brains out there had different ideas for me. In New York, even when I sang the double-meaninged lines written for *DuBarry Was a Lady*, I was still the wide-eyed type. I was in love with Bert Lahr in that show, wasn't I? That should have been enough to prove me wide-eyed. I *do* love Bert, but his features are not exactly classical, his face is not exactly sexy.

It's fundamental in show biz that an audience only cares about "the girl who's in love with the fella." If you're just a friend of the heroine you're just a wall to bounce dialogue against; you might as well have stood at home. On the stage, if I wanted a fellow I got him. I was *the* girl. When I fell in love, the audience was pulling for me.

I bring this up because, in my early flickers, I wasn't even "the friend of the heroine." When the movie makers were through lousing up my roles, I was so close to being a "heavy"—which means an "old meanie"—I might as well have worn a Frankenstein's monster suit and a wig trimmed with wiggly rubber snakes.

It's a cliché (and a phony one at that) to say that how big the part is or how small it is doesn't make any difference. The people who spout this kind of nonsense tell you that Mae West banked a million with one line—"Come up and see me sometime" —and that George Raft became a star without opening his mouth. He just flipped a coin. They'll add that there's no such thing as a small part. There are only small actors. That's too pat—too easy.

The truth is that everybody who's connected with a movie in

any way takes a bow if the picture's a success. That even goes for the man who's in charge of the studio dining room. He feels that without him the picture wouldn't have been any good, and in a way he's right, for few people seem to realize that a big combination of elements goes into making a successful picture. Not only that, but there are psychological moments in show business that make for success or failure. Sometimes you walk in at the right time and get a part you never dreamed you were going to get and the part makes you a star. Whereas if you'd walked in a day earlier or even an hour later—nothing. Also, like on a football squad, your material is all-important.

I wasn't the only one who was burned by what Hollywood did to me. The writer Gilbert Seldes was so rawed up that he popped off about it this way: "The musical shows which Miss Merman makes wonderful are bought by Hollywood and someone ruins them there. Her looks, I gather, aren't what Hollywood absolutely needs. Her talent is rarely equaled."

I'd help establish a show as a Broadway hit; then a studio would snap it up for a thick bundle. Presently, when you saw the thing on the screen, you'd have hell's own time recognizing it. The only thing familiar about it was the title. Any other similarity was strictly coincidental.

My original stage lyrics were thought too broad for anybody with a mental age higher than seven. So they were prettied up. To the surprise of nobody except the movie makers, this took all the kick out of flip and sassy lyrics. People wondered what all the horn tooting and drum beating had been about when the show played Broadway.

Originally I went to Hollywood hopped up with optimism, eagerness, and ambition. I'm not noted for laziness or doing as little as I can get away with. I wanted to give each scene everything I had. I thought I was doing it. I didn't notice the looks passed from director to producer to cameraman and back again, but when I saw *We're Not Dressing* on the screen, I got it. They'd used a fraction of the footage I'd been in. The rest had been kicked around the cutting room until lost. The important names in the cast were contract players, the bread-and-butter winners of the lot. I was there only for the one picture. Naturally, if anybody was cut, it was I.

I was told that my one big number was junked "because it came at the end." To me, this was a new high in sappy reasoning. When I said so in my softest tones, it was explained to me that "it distracted the audience from the story."

I thought up an unladylike phrase for that, too, but I didn't use it.

My big number was called "The Animal in Me." It took weeks to film. They needed all that time to train forty elephants to stand in a circle while I sang, and lift their feet and trunks in unison like Rockettes. Well, their feet anyhow; I guess Rockettes don't have trunks. They probably just have cute fitted overnight bags, like the one Grace Kelly carried in *Rear Window*. There were kangaroos and other animals in that scene too; but after spending all that dough they tossed it out.

Paramount's ads for *We're Not Dressing* carried the statement: "Ethel Merman will always be remembered for her rendering of 'Eadie Was a Lady' in the Broadway show, *Take a Chance*." That was a weird one. If they were going to say anything, you'd think they'd have said: "Ethel Merman will always be remembered for her songs in the Paramount movie, *We're Not Dressing*." Then I got it. They couldn't say *that*. People would ask, "What songs?"

When *We're Not Dressing* played the Paramount in New York, my grandmother, Mary Gardner, was taken to see it. She'd been on hand for my first Broadway performance in *Girl Crazy*. She caught every new performance I gave after that, until she passed away in May 1935. When she saw *We're Not Dressing*, she was eighty-two and she was getting a little woozy-minded. She didn't realize that what she'd seen was only a movie, so she couldn't understand why she wasn't taken backstage to say hello to me in my dressing room. Every time she saw me after that she complained, "Ethel, your aunt May took me to see you, but she wouldn't bring me back to see you."

"I wasn't on the stage, Grandma," I'd tell her. "I was on the screen." She didn't get it. Maybe it was because so little of me was *on* the screen.

Scrapping the dancing elephants was just a sample. Not only was I cut out of some of the big musical numbers, I was out of some of my speaking scenes too. Every time I blinked, more of me wound up in the dustbin with the mice.

But even if the public would have held still for my New York stage lyrics in their original form, they never had a chance to find out. There were some happy little parties called censors, who made a living out of trying things out on their own "clean minds" before they let them be tried out on anyone else's clean mind. I'll never forget the fuss made about a scene in my movie *Kid*

Millions, starring Eddie Cantor. In this scene eight- or nine-year-old little kids were shown eating ice cream. When they shoved themselves away from the table, their tummies were bulging. The censors O.K.'d the overstuffed little boys but booted out the footage of the little girls. They thought the padding representing too much ice cream made them look pregnant. That kind of thinking is disgusting. If there'd been a ship's rail handy, I'd have run to it and hung my head over.

When I'd been in my second stage show, *George White's Scandals*, I'd seen Irving Berlin and said hello to him, but I didn't really get to know him until 1938, when I worked in his picture project, *Alexander's Ragtime Band*.

But I was still getting the business. I was still "the other girl," or "just featured," depending upon which term was the least revolting. To me they were equally repulsive. I was still being planted in front of chalk lines and told not to move around too much when I sang. Once more I knocked my brains out doing things that were chopped out of the picture. The film was half over before I appeared on the screen. Even after that you missed me if you looked away to slap at a gnat. But you didn't miss the star of this production, Alice Faye.

She was soft, kittenlike, and cuddly. She was also the studio's mint. Fox always seems to have somebody lined up like that. It's the funniest thing; you'd think they have a stockpile of curvy, blond cuties stacked on the back lot. And "stacked" is the word for it. Faye had the publicity boys practically talking to themselves and driving around tacking pictures of her on trees, telephone poles, and vacant sheds.

All this did was confuse me. Still another movie, *Anything Goes*, had been a spectacular success as a Broadway show. I ought to know. I'd been in it. So what happened? When Paramount decided to make a film out of it they changed it as much as possible. In New York I'd sung "I Get a Kick Out of You" to Billy Gaxton, standing at a bar, as a sort of prologue to the rest of the show. In the movie version I was strung up on a crescent moon on wires and I had not feathers but whole birds of paradise in my hair. I was smothered in a big chiffon gown, and I was flown around the stage with three hundred extras chasing under me.

Naturally that killed it. On Broadway it had been staged simply, with a bow to the way Fanny Brice stepped out and sang a song all by herself. Yet there were gents with pointed heads in the studio who asked, "What happened to the movie version of the song?"

Then and there I promised myself, *I'll never come back to Hollywood again unless I'm certain I can do something worth while.*

That's one of the reasons why I love Walter Lang. Walter is a nice guy anyhow, but the way he directed the two movies, *Call Me Madam* and *There's No Business Like Show Business*, won my foolish heart. Other directors had told me I was "too brassy," "too bouncy," "too gusty"; that I "projected too much." When I was in a picture I had to underplay it. But when Walter was ready to direct *Call Me Madam* he told me, "Get out there and be as brassy and as full of bounce and gusto as you want to. That's what zillions of people who saw you in the theater paid money to see."

124

And while I'm at it, I want to make a deep bow to Sol Siegel, producer of *Call Me Madam* and *There's No Business Like Show Business*. It was Siegel who was mainly responsible for my appearance in *Show Business*. He felt I was the perfect choice for the role.

Chapter Nine

Back in August of 1938, after making *Alexander's Ragtime Band,* I arrived in New York. I was standing in the doorway of the train at the Grand Central Terminal, showing my teeth at a publicity photographer from the Fox New York office, when all of a sudden the train began to back out of the station.

The lad with the flash bulbs and the fast shutter had said, "I think it would be good if I took one of you swinging the trainman's lantern." So I swung it. Apparently it was regarded as a real honest-to-John signal by the boys up front in the locomotive, for the train started to back into the yard. That picture landed in the papers all right—and why not? It looked as if I was getting the railroad version of the hook they used to yank people from the vaudeville stage.

The drum beaters in the Fox publicity department didn't let a thing like that die for lack of nourishment. A story cracked the papers that read: "As a result of Ethel Merman's signaling chore for the New York Central, that lady has been admitted to the Brotherhood of Railroad Trainmen." It was true, and I've got a gold card to prove it. When Alexander Whitney, president of the B.R.R.T., and one hundred representatives who were attending a wage conference in Chicago had my railroading activities called to their attention, they wired me an offer of honorary brotherhood.

Apparently Mr. Whitney and his little pals were aware of the fact that there was such a thing as publicity *too!*

But I hadn't come home just to swing lanterns or to help the Fox flacks grab newspaper space. I'd checked in to report to Vinton Freedley for another Broadway production. I heaved a sigh of relief. *This* racket I knew. *This* public was my public.

It was a racket that had its sidesplitting side. It might not seem so funny if you were in the middle, getting the squeeze, but after it was over you'd laugh your head off at something that had you hopping on the griddle like a drop of cold water in hot grease while it was going on.

For instance, take what happened to Howard Lindsay and Buck Crouse when they tried to sign Billy Gaxton and me for Vinton Freedley's next show, *Red, Hot and Blue*. What the writers of a stage musical do when they try to sell a male star on his part is to make him think he's going to be the Mr. Big in the cast, the important one; the one with the lion's share of the lines. At least that's the way they talk while they're describing it to him. Then they go to the woman star and make her feel that her part is the dominant one, the one about which the action revolves. This sort of flimflam is the expected thing in the theater.

Crouse and Lindsay told Billy Gaxton about the part they had in mind for him first. Billy listened.

When they were through, he asked. "What's Ethel playing?"

"Remember that girl we mentioned briefly back there?" they asked. "Ethel plays that girl. We're not surprised you've forgotten her. After all, her role is so small."

Then Howard and Buck rushed down to see me at the Paramount, where I was serving a term in vaudeville. They were in my dressing room telling me about my role, laying it on thick and building it up, when Gaxton walked in. I didn't know what had been going on between them, so I didn't know how funny it was when Billy appeared, and Buck and Howard *had* to keep on talking.

Howard had just said to me, "Then Gaxton does this," when he gulped and said in horrified tones, "Here comes Gaxton now!"

Howard and Buck couldn't afford to unsell me, so they had to keep on making my part sound good. Gaxton listened quietly. Then he walked out. He also walked out of the show. He didn't say he'd been double-crossed. He didn't say anything. He didn't sign anything either. In his place Vinton hired a comedian with an inferiority complex. His name was Bob Hope.

Howard and Buck couldn't find a good first act for *Red, Hot and Blue*. They worked and worked; in fact we stayed out of town a week longer than we would have ordinarily stayed because we didn't have a good first-act finale. Finally about the middle of the first week in New Haven they hit upon a good one. It wasn't much, just something that would make an audience applaud and go out willing to come back to see the second act. As I remember it, the finale was as simple as this. I was crying on Jimmy Durante's shoulder and Jimmy said, "Don't cry, please, don't cry. Don't be lugubrious." I stopped crying for a moment, looked at him, and asked, "What's lugubrious mean?" Jimmy looked at me blankly, then said, "Go ahead and cry."

To arrange for these lines, Howard and Buck felt that they had to get Bob Hope off stage. He'd been in all the other finales they'd tried but in this one they gave him an exit.

When he heard this, Hope's agent, "Doc" Louis Shurr, came up to see Buck and Howard and said, "Boys, you're going to hurt the show."

"How do you mean?" they asked.

"I mean with Hope out of the finale," Louis said.

"Look, Shurr," they said, "we've been sweating our heads off for weeks trying to get a good finale and we've found one. We don't care whether Hope's in the finale or out of it. It's a good enough finale for us and that's the way it's going to be."

"I've been with Bob a long time," Louis protested. "He's going to feel bad about this. He'll go on depressed and if he's not in that finale maybe he won't be able to give a good performance."

Louis was very persuasive. In the meantime Howard's mind was working. He was thinking, *Oh well, if he wants to be on the stage we can bring him back. We can work that out.* Buck's mind was working along the same line but neither of them said anything to Shurr. They wanted to consult each other first. So they said, "Hope is out of the finale. That's all there is to it. He's out."

129

"All right boys," Doc Shurr said and went away.

The minute he'd shut the door Buck and Howard looked at each other and Howard said, "We could get him in the finale if that's all he wants. When Durante says, 'Don't cry,' we can let Hope say, 'No, don't cry,' so he can be there, standing on stage."

"Fine, let's let him do that," Buck said. "We'd better let him know right away." So they called a restaurant across the street and got him.

"Hello, Bob," Buck said. "Doc tells me you feel bad about not being in the finale."

"As a matter of fact I do," Bob said. "After all, Jimmy, Ethel, and I are three stars together, aren't we?"

"O.K., Bob," Buck and Howard said. "You're in the finale."

"Thanks," Bob said, "that's great!" and he hung up and went back to his table.

Doc Shurr hadn't dared go to the restaurant where Bob was for a while. He walked around New Haven thinking, *How can I face Bob?* It wasn't until a half hour later that he got up enough courage to break the sad news. He walked into the restaurant. There was Hope being the life of the party. He went up to Bob's table, sat down, and looked at Bob pityingly. Finally Doc said, "Afraid I've got some bad news for you, Bob. You're not in the finale."

"I am too in the finale," Bob said, and went on laughing.

"But, Bob," Doc said, "I've been over to see Howard and Buck and you're not in the finale."

"Yes, I am," Bob said. "I am so in the finale!"

They had a lot of trouble getting together on the same wave

130

length. Those who overheard them said later that their dialogue was better than most of the lines Howard and Buck had written for the show.

Howard and Buck have still another story about me they seem to think humorous although some of their stories about me don't seem funny to me at all. They were in London once when I was there with Pop and Mom. They were trying to decide upon a comedian for *Red, Hot and Blue.* At one time or another they wrote the show for five different comedians. Maybe that's one of the things that was wrong with it.

Pop became ill when I was there and one night when I ran into Buck and Howard I told them how worried I was about him. "But I think he'll be all right," I said. "I've got the King's own doctor for him. *He* ought to be pretty good, oughtn't he, holding down a job like that?"

Buck and Howard offer it as a sidesplitting Merman remark. See what I mean? What's so funny about that?

Red, Hot and Blue didn't have much of a book. The New York *Time's* Brooks Atkinson said that the authors would probably be pleased if he didn't mention their libretto at all, since the connecting links of the story consisted mainly of "Oh, hello, Bob's" and "I was looking for you's."

For some reason which escapes me now, I was running a contest in the show and in the contest a girl who had a waffle mark on her behind was supposed to win a prize. The problem of testing a number of girls for such a mark, without having the Boston Watch and Ward Society running a blood pressure about the necessity for peering here and peering there on the girls' anatomies,

131

took some working out. Jimmy Durante thought of a way to do it. The girls were dressed in skirts made of material with two-way visibility and when the lights were turned on in a certain way you could see through them.

The action was laid in Washington and it bore a prophetic resemblance to *Call Me Madam*, except that *Call Me Madam* was to be a better show when it came along. My role was that of a manicurist Bob Hope had promoted into being Washington's leading hostess. For some reason Hope had been up to Sing Sing to entertain, and, having seen the captain of the prison polo team (Jimmy Durante)—who was being sprung shortly—had hired him as his secretary. When he made his entrance, Jimmy's polo mallet and polo outfit were covered with prison stripes. In another scene, Jimmy was a witness before a congressional committee. He didn't trust the committee's lawyers, so he insisted on examining himself.

To flash back for a moment, Vinton Freedley had had a terrible time getting *Red, Hot and Blue* off the ground. He signed me first. Then he tried to get a firm commitment from Jimmy Durante, but Jimmy was roaming around in Italy so his business manager, Lou Clayton, signed for him.

It was then that the famed Battle of the Billing occurred. This battle featured my agent, Lou Irwin, and Lou Clayton, Durante's representative. For the first and only time in their lives these two gents—who never forgot *anything*—had forgotten to specify who was to get top billing in the contracts they negotiated for their respective principals. Freedley couldn't have cared less, but the two agents cared like crazy. If it had got around that they'd forgotten a billing clause, it would have made them seem very absent-minded.

When the rhubarb about the billing was at its hottest, Freedley said that if he could only reach Jimmy by transatlantic telephone he was sure he could straighten things out, so he asked Clayton where Jimmy was.

"I think he's in a place called Rome Capri," Clayton said vaguely.

Freedley say up until five o'clock in the morning getting the American Embassy in Italy on the phone. When he got through he said, "This is Vinton Freedley in New York. Do you know if there's a comedian named Durante traveling around in Italy somewhere?"

"He was here," the spokesman at the embassy said. "But he's in Capri now." So Clayton was half right anyhow.

Freedley called Jimmy in Capri and said, "We're having trouble with the billing. Get right on the *Deutschland* and come home. It leaves from Hamburg."

"Not me!" Jimmy said. "I won't fly."

He'd decided that the S.S. *Deutschland* was a dirigible. It cost Vinton forty dollars to explain that it was a passenger ship.

When Jimmy came home, he was sweet about the billing, as he always is. "As long as I'm good on the stage, I don't care," he said. But Clayton still balked. I was rehearsing, Jimmy was rehearsing, and Clayton and Irwin were hollering and banging on Freedley's desk. There were days when we didn't know whether the show would open or not.

As I recall it, to Cole Porter goes the credit for thinking up

133

the compromise that saved the day. It was a crisscross arrangement of names like this:

You'd think that would have ended it, but it only partly satisfied the competing strategists, because my agent and Durante's agent asked, "Will the public read the one going down first, or will they read the one going up first?" So it had to be changed every two weeks.

Cole Porter is not only a genius at writing songs, composing music, and working out trick arrangements of names to keep managers and agents happy; he's a genius at the art of sophisticated living, too; at least, he seems that way to me. When he orders wine, he sends it back if it's not exactly the right temperature. If you have lunch with him in his patio, a menu is written out and stuck in a transparent plastic thing before you. You sit there and look at your menu, and Cole looks at his, and there's pleasant table talk.

I'm not a girl who cares whether the wine's the right temperature or not. If somebody doesn't like it, O.K.; let's take it and pour it in the sink and go on down to the corner drugstore.

I'm no connoisseur. I don't eat potatoes—too starchy—but if I did, I'd be a meat-and-potatoes girl. If I go to a fancy restaurant where the other customers are insisting the sauce has got to be this or got to be that, I just tell the man, "Bring me some consommé, two lamb chops, and some asparagus with butter sauce." Full stop. Period.

Regardless of story weaknesses, Cole had some good songs in *Red, Hot and Blue*. I sang a song with Hope called "It's De-Lovely," and I sang another song, "Ridin' High."

Cole writes with a tempo and a rhythm that can't be beat for dancing. It's my guess that you hear Porter five to one to anyone else's dance music in night clubs. The same thing is pretty much true with singers; more of Porter's songs are sung in night clubs than anybody else's. For instance, seven out of the twelve songs Billy Daniels sang at the Mocambo last year were Porter songs.

One day Roberto Hope took it into his head to sing "It's De-Lovely" lying down. He lay down by the footlights, with me standing behind him. I controlled myself with an effort that almost busted my stay strings, but afterward I had a heart-to-heart talk with Freedley.

"If that so-called comedian ever does that again," I said, tight-lipped but ladylike, "I'm going to plant my foot on his kisser and leave more of a curve in his nose than nature gave it."

Vinton must have passed a few of the calmer passages of our discussion along to pal Bob. All I know is he never did it again.

Jimmy Durante was easy to work with. He learned his lines by having them read to him by the well-known dramatic coach and Shakespearean student, Professor Eddie Jackson, of Clayton, Jackson, and Durante. Eddie gave Jimmy his private version of Little Theater technique; then Jimmy gave it his own individual touch. His big contribution was to pronounce difficult words in a Durante-ish way. It was quite a contribution.

Hope would almost rather kid me and break me up and get the

chorus girls—or anybody else on the stage—to laughing than he would make the audience laugh.

Several months after *Red, Hot and Blue* was over and done with, Buck and Howard went out to Paramount at the time when Hope's first picture was opening in Los Angeles. It was very successful.

Bob ran into them the next day on the Paramount lot and he asked, "Did you see the opening of my picture last night?"

Buck said, "No, we're putting off seeing it until tomorrow night so we can catch your ad-libbing."

In *Red, Hot and Blue*, I also sang a torchy Cole Porter number called "Down in the Depths, on the Ninetieth Floor." Vinton Freedley had had a gold lamé gown made for me to wear when I sang this ditty, standing alone in a golden spotlight. When I turned around, the audience could see that I was wearing a bustle consisting of a nest with a hen on it. It was Vinton's idea of a riotous sight gag.

It fetched a belly laugh all right, which was what Vinton wanted, but it wasn't what I wanted. I'm all for rowdy hilarity; I've contributed my share of it to the world, but there I was, singing my heart out, and what was I getting? Guffaws. To me, they spoiled the torchiness.

I told Vinton, "That nest comes off. Any audience that gets a laugh out of me gets it while I'm looking at them." A little light mowing with a pair of scissors in my dressing room fixed everything.

That crack of mine—" 'Any audience that gets a laugh out of me gets it while I'm looking at them,' " coupled with "a little

136

light mowing with a pair of scissors"—makes me think of the present condition of my hair (although I know this is going off on a tangent). Last August, the day after they stopped shooting *There's No Business Like Show Business*, I had the part of my mop I wore tucked up at the back of my neck cut off and all those curls, that used to take hours to do, removed. I must say that I'm much more comfortable now, and I feel chic and very *pomme de terre*. But I still look like me from in front. That's the selling side—the side that's my trade mark. Would RCA Victor trade its trade mark for a French poodle with its ear cocked at the horn?

After that "flag on the play," as the football sportscasters say, I'll get back to *Red, Hot and Blue*, which in turn brings me to one of my best friends, Lew Kessler. Lew is one of the most talented pianists I know. When I'm booked to do a show in or near New York, I'm uneasy unless Lew's perched on the piano stool making the keys talk the way I understand. I met him first when I was in *Red, Hot and Blue*. He'd played piano previously for Cole Porter, so Cole handed him a sheaf of music and told him, "You're going to work my new show. Take this, teach the people, and find their keys." He meant find what key the song had to be played in for each principal.

I've heard Lew describe that first time we worked together. When he tells it, it goes like this: "I'd never had any experience with Mermo." (He calls me Mermo; Dorothy Fields calls me Mermsy, Merm, or sometimes Stinky; and Georgie Solotaire calls me The Merm.) "But I'd heard she was a whip with a quip, and if you weren't used to her, she'd leave you bruised. The first day I worked with her in the Alvin Theater, I'd been given this number to work over with her. I don't remember what key she said she wanted it in, but I do remember it was hard to transpose into. What's more, I'd never looked at the music before."

When Lew gets to this part of his story, I barge in myself with a detail or two. The key must have been the key of B. I never go for anything higher than a middle C. If anybody wants me to go higher than that in a show song, I tell them, "I should tear my lungs out? Remember, I'm going to have to do this every night in the week for a year or more. Not only that, but I've got a lot of other songs to sing. And between songs I have lines to say."

I could go to a D if I have to, but I get just as much effect out of making C my top note—and with less strain. Most singers get very enthusiastic about themselves when they hit a top note in practice and it sounds good, but after they've done it for two months, six nights a week plus two matinees, they end up by asking to have it transposed lower. Me, I wind up in the same key in which I started. Anyhow, the transposition I wanted Lew to do for me was into the key of B. B has five sharps, which made it difficult to play the first time he tried transposing it, and he fumbled it a bit.

The way Lew goes on with his story is this: "Those five sharps were murder; Ethel was singing in the key I was playing in all right, but I wasn't playing the right harmony. When she got through, she turned to me and said, 'Look, pal, do me a favor. Take the Vienna rolls off your fingers!'"

Lew says, "I wasn't very experienced in show business, but I discovered one thing: if you meet Merman when you first start, after that everything is baby talk. With this woman, you never know what she's going to say, but if you have stamina, she's wonderful."

I have a bigger vocal range than usual. I can sing from low G up to the three or four and a half notes over an octave. Most people think it's a big range if they can sing one and a half notes over an octave.

Donald O'Connor, who's been with me in two films, complains at the amount of volume my pipes generate. He says that the first day he got up to sing a duet with me, we were standing side by side making a studio recording which would afterward appear on a sound track. I had an earphone on one of my ears and Donald had one on his right ear. When we'd run through the thing, we got a playback through the earphones so we could make up our minds whether we were satisfied with the result or not. We kept the other ear free so we could hear each other sing while the recording was being made.

Donald said afterward that he wished there were some way he could have plugged his free ear with cotton, because I brought forth a note that bent his eardrum so badly he couldn't hear out of it properly for two days.

On the other hand, I was at Arthur Schwartz's house one night at a party and I must not have been in very good voice. A friend of Arthur's, a woman who didn't want to come to the party at all, was on deck. She'd just gotten off a plane after a long and trying journey, but Arthur had begged her to come anyhow and she sat in this room with a bunch of us. I started singing at one-thirty in the morning, and although I was only ten feet away from her, this woman fell asleep. Either she was the tiredest woman who ever lived or I had an off night. Or the airplane ride had made her temporarily deef. Probably the latter.

Still and all, I had enough volume to be chosen to sing the campaign song when Franklin Delano Roosevelt was nominated for governor of New York State. I sang on the same program with him.

I also sang at the dedication of the liner *Normandie*, in 1935. In appreciation, the French consul gave me a pass for a voyage to Europe and back. I took Pop and Mom along but, as I've already mentioned, Pop got sick on shipboard and was in a hospital in London all the time I was in England. I had to hurry back to Broadway to do a show, so although I crossed the ocean both ways I didn't see anything of Europe because of Pop's illness.

They gave my agent, Lou Irwin, a pass on the French Line, too, but he didn't use it at that time. Twenty years later, I understand that Lou wrote to the steamship company to ask, "I have a pass on your line, can I still use it?" They wrote back, "Sure, go ahead. Any time."

While I'm on the subject of Lou, we finally drifted apart when my contract with him expired. I didn't renew it. He'd gone to Hollywood to open an office and I was still in New York. He figured that his New York representative could handle my affairs, but I couldn't see it that way. A "New York representative" wasn't Lou. If I had a contract with Lou I wanted Lou himself.

Lou handles some of the biggest people in the profession and they're happy with him—people like Peter Lind Hayes and Mary

Healy, and the Ritz Brothers; but I think my reasons for parting with him were understandable.

Red, Hot and Blue ran for forty weeks in New York before moving on to Chicago, but with any kind of break it might have run forty more. When it opened in Chicago, it was just blue; it wasn't hot. Vinton Freedley had ordered seventy tons of sand to be loaded into sandbags to counterbalance the scenery, so it could be raised and lowered, but the house carpenter didn't believe any show would need seventy tons, so he'd ordered seven. At eight o'clock on the first night everybody was ready to go, when the scenery stuck four feet above the stage.

The stage hands chinned themselves on it, but it wouldn't budge and Freedley sent Jimmy Durante out to explain things to the audience. I'm glad I didn't have to do it!

A ticket mess like that doesn't mean that two groups of people had seats for the next night, as you might think. The *second* group doesn't see the show. The first-nighters come back. You see, the ticket is not dated. It just says "first night." So whatever the opening night is, that's the night those tickets are good for. They try to take care of the second-night people later.

The show never recovered from that initial setback. But the fact that it didn't run on and on and on in Chicago wasn't hard for me to take. Being away from home was not for me. I never did like the road. Even if I'd been in New York I'd have tried to duck going to the theater and working during the prickly-heat days. I'd have stayed at home in my apartment where there was a breeze. Most important of all, I'd have had the comforting knowledge that I was at home in my own city. When you're uncomfortable in a strange town, you're twice as uncomfortable.

Chapter Ten

Almost all of the shows with which I've been connected were hits. One exception was *Stars in Your Eyes.* This is hard for me to figure, since Dorothy Fields wrote the lyrics, Arthur Schwartz wrote the music, Dwight Deere Wiman produced it, and the cast was tops. It included Jimmy Durante, Richard Carlson, and Tamara Toumanova, the ballerina.

Toumanova's agent was a guy named Milton Bender. Arthur Schwartz and Dorothy Fields and Dwight Deere Wiman hired Toumanova because they wanted her kind of dancing in the show. They knew she had never acted and they knew that her English, while charming, would be cloudy. That part of it was a gamble. But all through rehearsal Bender kept assuring them that Toumanova was going to be terrific. "Don't worry, fellows!" he kept saying. "She'll be great! I know!" He was Mr. Confidence himself. He looked like a betting man who'd got a tip from a talking horse.

On opening night in New Haven, Wiman and the others were bright enough to protect Toumanova's first appearance by giving her a dancing entrance, in which she could show her big style right away. She socked her act over the footlights with authority. She wore class like a leotard. When the applause finally subsided, Bender turned to those of us who were standing backstage and said, with a sigh of relief that came from under the boards, "I said she was great, didn't I, and *now* I believe it."

It was the most typically agency remark I've ever heard. No wonder he was stupefied with amazement. Imagine an agent's client being anywhere near as good as he'd said she was.

Stars in Your Eyes made its getaway in 1939, but it was bumped and jostled going around the turns. It hung on for six months, but six months wasn't long enough to get a production that expensive off the nut.

This is how *Stars in Your Eyes* happened. Arthur Schwartz told me about it. He had no show and he was sitting trying to think of an idea for one and he thought, *What would happen if a liberal song writer, like Harold Jacob Rome, who wrote* Pins and Needles, *became so famous that he was sent for by Darryl Zanuck and offered a job?* Pins and Needles was substantially a revue, but the characters were workers in the garment business. It was a very successful revue, it wasn't Communistic at all—certainly nobody ever accused it of that—it was merely written from a union point of view.

Arthur became all fascinated with this question of what would

happen if a fellow like that got involved with Darryl Zanuck because Zanuck kept telling him, "You're great." It wasn't likely
that this would actually happen of course, so it would only be a
satire on Hollywood.

Arthur watered this story germ for a few weeks to see whether
he could make it sprout. Then he tried it out on J. P. McEvoy,
who was then a writer of musical shows among other things, but
who is now a roving reporter for the *Reader's Digest*.

McEvoy was in California at the time—he was writing Shirley
Temple pictures for Fox—so Arthur called him up and asked, "I
want to know if you want to do a show." McEvoy said he thought
he would. Arthur mailed him a crude synopsis of twenty or thirty
pages and J.P. thought the idea would make a great show, so he
came East and worked with Arthur for a while, and Arthur got
Dorothy Fields in on it too. Arthur called her from New York
direct to her mud bath in the Arrowhead Springs Hotel in California. They have phones right in the mud bath and Arthur told
her a little about his ideas, so she came East too, after canceling
whatever plans she had, including the bath.

All three of them started to work without having a real setup.
All they had was the bones of a plot. Then came the question of
finding a cast. Dorothy knew me personally. In fact she was a
very good friend of mine. She got me interested and they got
Durante interested too.

Durante was in New York, playing a night club that had begun
life as the Earl Carroll Theater. I remember going there to see a
guy who wore mostly gold paint dance on a big drum to Ravel's
"Bolero." Maybe you already know George Kaufman's famous

144

crack about that theater. If you don't it goes like this. Carroll opened it with one of his revues, which were pretty abhorrent to fellows like Kaufman, but George went to the opening night anyhow for some reason, perhaps because it happened to be the opening night of the theater itself as well as the show.

Next day a friend of his asked him, "What did you think of that theater last night? I saw you there."

"I couldn't tell," George said. "I saw it under very disadvantageous circumstances. The curtain was up."

That's where Jimmy was playing.

Arthur offers a side light on Jimmy that is typical of my large-schnozzed pal. He remembers going with Jimmy's business manager, Lou Clayton, to see Jimmy at the hotel on Broadway where Jimmy had his permanent suite when he was in New York. It was located on the second floor on the corner.

Arthur asked him why he liked it there. After all, the noise was slightly deafening and you couldn't hear yourself talk, in that second story, on a Broadway corner. I can't do a Durante imitation, but what Jimmy told Arthur was, "I love to see the people goin' up and down Broadway late at night when I come home, and I like to see 'em on a Sunday night changin' the billin' on the Loew's State. Changin' that billin', takin' those letters down, and puttin' those new letters up. You can't get nuttin' more excitin' than that!"

Jimmy called Arthur "Artur"; and he called me "Etel."

There was so much talent in that show it's a wonder that it's not running still, although some of the talent hadn't been really discovered. Dan Dailey was in it, and Jerome Robbins and Nora

Kaye were chorus dancers. But it didn't get the long run it should have had. Jimmy Durante's theory was that we'd made a mistake in opening in New Haven on Friday the thirteenth. "We oughta put it off till Monday," he said, shaking his nose.

Shows usually opened on a Thursday in New Haven—they played half a week there—but we had quite a complicated production and could only open one night later than usual.

Everybody had his own explanation for that short run. Lee Shubert's theory was that certain members of the cast were being paid too much. Arthur Schwartz thought that there was something about the show that was wrong from the public's point of view, only he couldn't figure what it was. Arthur's theory is that no show fails if enough people recommend it to their friends when they leave the theater. "I have seen shows I've hated become great successes," he says, "and vice versa. I've seen shows that I loved become failures. Right now there are several shows running in New York which are doing sensational business and I can't explain it except by saying that a lot of the public which goes to those shows comes out saying, 'I'm going to tell my friends about this.'"

When Oscar Hammerstein was busy preparing the show *Me and Juliet,* he was walking up and down in a hallway talking to Arthur Schwartz. During their conversation he said that he figured that every person who goes to see a New York stage show will see twenty other people within a week's time, and he'll mention the show to them. He'll either say he has seen a wonderful show, he's seen a medium good show, or he's seen a lousy show. So if it's a great show, like a *South Pacific,* everybody who's there on one night—there are 1700 seats in the Majestic Theater—means that 1700 times 20, or 34,000, people will be told within the next few days, "You gotta go to see *South Pacific*."

Where Oscar got that figure twenty from I don't know; maybe he did a little research. But by and large I agree with him. I don't think that anything governs the success or failure of a show (including the critics) as much as whether the audience buys it or not. If it buys it, it'll sell it to future audiences.

The lead male character of *Stars in Your Eyes* was played by the Abbey Theatre's loss to America, Jimmy Durante. Jimmy lugged a collapsible polo mallet around with him on stage. Every once in a while it folded or came apart and sawdust spurted from it. When that occurred, Durante explained, "Toimites!"

Jimmy was supposed to be a studio idea man who walked around and had ideas, big thoughts, money-making flashes. There are several characters like that in Hollywood. There is one at Metro who is called Hopkins—his nickname is Hobby. And there were others on other lots. Hobby has had several of his ideas produced at Metro through the years. One of them, the most walloping of all so far as success was concerned, was when he tapped a passing producer on the shoulder and said, "Gable, Jeanette Mac-Donald, San Francisco earthquake? That's all."

Metro made it and I don't have to tell you how the gold rolled in.

In the story of *Stars in Your Eyes* Jimmy was a Hobby-type man. The part of the head of the studio was played by Robert Ross, who recently died. In our show he was called The Czar of All the Rushes.

147

A great director, Josh Logan, directed the thing. It was the first time I'd worked with Josh but he must have thought I had possibilities, because, after the show opened, he gave me a silver cup. Engraved on it was: "To Sarah Bernhardt, Jr., from Josh." I keep it in my curio cabinet at home, where I stick the things I treasure most. That inscription was laying it on pretty thick, but I didn't simper and protest, "Gosh, Josh, you shouldn't have done that!" Even if it wasn't true, it was something to live up to.

When I asked Josh to help me remember stuff for this story, he was in the middle of rehearsing his show *Fanny*. Nobody can concentrate more on the job at hand than Josh when he's in rehearsal, but irregardless, he took time out to write me a long letter about our association together. "My first remembrance of you is in *Stars in Your Eyes*," he wrote. "Everyone had told me you were a good singer, but not much of an actress. So it was a surprise to me to find out that you were an instinctive actress. I did suggest a few bits of business here and there, but I didn't have to teach them to you. All I had to do was illustrate them and you had them."

I don't think that anybody will ever get me mixed up with Duse or Bernhardt, but Josh meant I'm better than adequate, and if it's true that I can do a little acting I don't know who's around to crowd me in my particular field. In fact, that field has broadened and it shouldn't be necessary to cast me as the mother of children like Donald O'Connor and Mitzi Gaynor in future pictures. I could have a ball playing a gutsy, bouncy, broad-comedy character like a slimmer Marie Dressler. For that matter, Marie did musicals at one time, so that's one channel I can move into.

Stars in Your Eyes was the first show in which I'd been given a part in which I had solid scenes as a comic. One scene J. P. McEvoy wrote was a classic I've heard Josh Logan tell people, "I'll never forget the seduction scene in *Stars in Your Eyes*, the one in which Ethel and Dick Carlson got together in her portable dressing room." That Josh Logan is my boy!

In that scene I was a famous movie siren who was pitching woo to her handsome but too innocent young leading man. I plied this hard-to-get dreamboat with strong waters. Finally he got himself a snootful and came to rest on the couch beside me. He was just leaning over to embrace me when he saw a copy of *Alice in Wonderland* on a shelf and with loud yelps of joy he announced it was his favorite book. He asked me to read it aloud to him. The episode ended with my opening the book and saying in a strangled voice: "Chapter One. Down the Rabbit Hole!"

When I read, "Alice was getting very tired of sitting by her sister with nothing to do," the audience screamed.

Then the lights went out to denote a time lapse. When they came on again, I was still reading, with a scowl on my face. I looked at my young man, and with all the venom I could squirt into it, I said, "Chapter Eleven! Who Stole the Tarts?" That really fractured the people.

Presently the mood of the scene changed. This new mood had me perched on a table near a pilot light, alone on an empty sound stage. I was beginning to realize that I was going to have to buy my young man with presents and fat roles because I couldn't make him love me in any other way. So I sang a song (with Dorothy Fields's lyrics) in a voice that had died inside of me before it came out. In the song I told my young man that he owed me nothing and that, while I might be headed for an enormous wreck, it was my party and I'd pay the check. That song got the audience on my side, and for the first time they began to sympathize with me.

To detour for just a moment, I once had a frustration in real life like that. In August 1943 the papers reported: "When Ethel Merman cut a birthday cake at the Stage Door Canteen last night, the recipient, a six-foot marine, refused to kiss her. 'I got married Wednesday,' he said. 'I ain't going to kiss nobody this week.'"

I should have made it a week later. That leatherneck looked like Bob Mathias, the Olympic champion.

In *Stars in Your Eyes*, Jimmy Durante and I had a hilarious duet called "It's All Yours." We came out in Russian costumes, wearing big Cossack hats, and flapped around in furs trimmed with ermine. But our Russky trimmings had nothing to do with the song. Its theme was, "It's all yours, everything you see!"

With the word "see," Jimmy took his fur hat and whapped it down into the orchestra pit. The sheet music took off like sea gulls flying, and a lot of the music stands toppled over. In the midst of all this confusion, we interpolated Durante-type jokes.

"Stop the music, stop the music!" Jimmy barked like a seal. "Don't raise the bridge, boys; lower the river!" Then he went on with the song, "It's all yours . . ."

It was mad.

Or Jimmy would ask, "What do you think of a house with no basement?" And he'd answer himself, "I think it's low."

I'd been given things to interpolate too. "Ethel," Jimmy would ask, "does this bus go over the Queensboro Bridge?"

"Well, if it don't we're all going to get a hell of a duckin'," I'd say.

Jimmy cackled, slapped his thighs, and we both laughed like crazy.

He'd say, "I was walking down the street and a bunch of kids followed me. A policeman stopped me and asked, 'What have you done?' and I said, 'I ain't done nuttin'!' And he said, 'You must have done somethin' to have all of those kids followin' you.'" End of joke. That one was triple-distilled, 100 per cent Durante. It may seem strictly shaggy-dog, but with Jimmy doing it, it was convulsing.

But to get back to the mutual-admiration thing between Josh and me, Josh doesn't think me perfect by any means. In fact there was something I didn't like to do that bothered him. When a show had been running for a while, he'd call a "refresher rehearsal." Sometimes the cast begin to fluff their lines, or grow careless, or not put as much crispness into what they're doing as they did when the show was new. During the first months of a run, the producer or director (or both) slip quietly into the theater (the sneaks), sit in a rear row, and make notes about who's flubbing the clutch. Then they go out muttering to themselves, "Nothing can slip as fast as a show!" or "Actors and actresses never seem to realize when they're letting down."

So a rehearsal is called "to jack things up"; and the director stands up and says, "I've made a few notes. In the second scene you didn't do so-and-so. You lost your laugh. For six months you got a boff in this spot, but now you've lost it three nights in a row."

I resented this because I always did it exactly as I'd done it opening night, and everybody admitted I did. I went to those refresher courses but I went dragging my feet.

The year of *Stars in Your Eyes* was also the year of the New York World's Fair. That fair siphoned most of the entertainment dollars from New York out to Flushing, Long Island. The transients we'd counted on to fill our theater flocked out to see the Trylon, the Perisphere, and Billy Rose's Aquacade. Maybe if we could have got the audiences up there on the stage instead of us, and they had had as much fun as we had, and we could have sat out front—or sneaked out to see Johnny Weissmuller and Eleanor Holm at the Aquacade—*Stars in Your Eyes* would have run as long as *Oklahoma!* or *South Pacific*.

Among my souvenirs of *Stars in Your Eyes* was a bouquet tossed to me by one reviewer: "In addition to her well-established ability to hold one note and shake her bracelets, Ethel Merman displays such a firm grasp of the art of comic acting that she practically has it by the throat."

Am I wrong or was there a brickbat concealed in that bouquet?

Pasted carefully into one of the scrapbooks my pop has kept for me is another souvenir, my first newspaper interview. I gave it to a dark, hairy, half-pint young man named Sidney Skolsky after I opened in *Girl Crazy*. Not long ago I got that interview out and gave it a gander. It was interesting to read over again after all the years between. Part of the Ethel Merman that comes through in that column has changed; the rest of her is pretty much the same.

I told Skolsky that I was five feet six and a quarter inches tall and weighed one hundred and twenty-one pounds; that I had brown eyes, brown hair, and a large brown mole on my left arm. I also told him that my nickname was "Zimmie," that my favorite expression was "a-raz-ma-taza," and that I collected novelties for my bedroom, and the room was thick with artificial dogs, dolls, and silk rabbits. I was very fond of lamps—I had five in my bedroom—and I often slept with my light on.

"She's still a big kid and still hollers for her mother," Skolsky wrote. "Say something mean to her and she'll start to bawl. Red is her favorite color. She likes to wear a dress the color of her fingernails. Wears only peach-colored underwear.

"She has taken a photograph of every marquee on which her name was spelled out," Sidney went on. "She sleeps on her left side and faces the window. With her head on the side, she tries to lie on her stomach. It's quite a trick. Her ambition is to be a dramatic actress. Getting her body suntanned is one of her hobbies. Almost daily she journeys to the roof of the house for a sunbath. Her pet is a fox terrier called Beauty. Beauty was before Scrapsie. He's fifteen years old and he looks like a cow. When she's away from home she writes postal cards to her dog.

Skolsky didn't mention the other sayings I favored at that time. I used them a lot, then dropped them. Two of them were "Friends say my voice is promising, but I don't trust promises" and "Fun comes in bunches, like bananas."

153

One of the high points of my life was the First Gershwin Memorial Concert at Lewisohn Stadium. I won't ever forget it if I live to be a million. When I was asked to be in this concert in memory of George, the program shaped up like this: It began with a selection from *Strike Up the Band,* conducted by Ferde Grofé. Then came "An American in Paris," conducted by Alexander Smallens. After that I sang three solos with Ferde Grofé conducting. Last of all came "Rhapsody in Blue," with Harry Kauffman as pianist.

Like a lot of things that turn out O.K., the dry runs before this concert bubbled with trouble. Just before I rehearsed with the Philharmonic, somebody discovered that there were only enough orchestrations for a pit band. There were no orchestrations for a whole symphonic orchestra and, after all, just a piano, a trumpet, a sax, and traps, etc., wouldn't be quite enough. This stumped the musicians. Then someone phoned Frank Black and asked him to dash off a hundred-odd orchestrations and Black said Ferde Grofé was the guy for the job. Ferde went into a huddle with himself, came up with a complete arrangement, and although they were mere babes in the jazz woods, some of the symphonic musicians copied the orchestrations and passed the sheets around to the men of the Philharmonic.

It was next discovered that I didn't sing the three Gershwin songs I was scheduled to sing—"The Man I Love," "They Can't Take That Away from Me," and "I Got Rhythm," in the key in which they'd been written. For example, I sang "I Got Rhythm" in F, while the standard orchestrations were in another key, and since I didn't sing in that key other orchestrations had to be made in a special key.

All this trouble and tribulation were not in my department. All I know is they asked me to sing and I sang.

And when I'd sung "I Got Rhythm," I had to do it over again, for when I was all through I heard a tapping sound. I looked around. The violinists were tapping their bows on their violins. It seems that if musicians are pleased with an artist that's their way of applauding. It's a rare compliment. They don't do it often.

After all, I was a blues singer, and these men were accustomed to accompanying serious types. But they weren't applauding me because I was wearing white crepe and white fox with gold ornaments; it was their way of telling me that they thought me a pro, and I was touched.

When I sang "I Got Rhythm" at the Lewisohn Stadium, I forgot I was appearing in dignified surroundings and just let them

155

have it. I must have really torn loose, judging by the clipping somebody sent me from the Pittsburgh *Post-Gazette*. "When Ethel Agnes Zimmermann, the girl with a twinkling eye, appeared last night in New York's Lewisohn Stadium," the clipping said. "Miss Merman rose to new heights on the wings of Gershwin song. . . . She sang 'I Got Rhythm' the way a beminked and manicured audience liked it. Any rendering of music by the late George Gershwin would be incomplete without her." (That slap on the back meant a lot to me. Since then I've always referred to that paper as "the good old *Post-Gazette*.")

After the concert I told friends that while the Philharmonic was big at Bach, Beethoven, and Brahms, and while I loved each and every one of them as people, they were squares when it came to jazz. It didn't take me long to discover that a Philharmonic pace is slower than the pace set by a Broadway-show pit band. I tried to pull a hundred symphoners along with me at the tempo I was used to and I felt that I was carrying a hundred men on my shoulders.

To shift from commercial into artistic, the point has been made that there are two kinds of burlesque shows. One of them is coarse and stupid and the other is coarse and funny. Although my next show, *DuBarry Was a Lady*, had its burlesquey moments, it was funny and smart; even funny and elegant.

DuBarry was based on a goofy idea. Bert Lahr was cast as a washroom attendant at 21 who'd won a lottery ticket. He was in love with a night club star—me. I was very sweet to him, but I didn't think him romantic. I mean, after all, he was a washroom worker, wasn't he? In the *DuBarry* story, someone slipped

Bert a micky and he dreamed he was back in the days of Du-Barry. There we were in the French court and I'm playing Madame DuBarry, and Bert is playing my lover.

There was a scene where he chased me around a bedroom like Wes Santee in an indoor track meet in Madison Square Garden and there was a comedy scene where he was shot by an arrow where his satin trousers were tightest and they had to send for the doctor to remove the arrow. It was one of the most hilarious shows ever produced on Broadway, and as anyone can see it was also very *théâtre intime* and Moscow Art Theaterish. Not to kick it around any longer, Madame DuBarry gave room for some real Frenchy situations in a broad, earthy kind of way.

Bert had just finished doing *The Wizard of Oz*, but for some reason Metro-Goldwyn-Mayer didn't take up his option. As Bert explained it, "After all, how many Cowardly Lion parts can you play?"

Buddy De Sylva had plenty of money of his own, and this made him feel independent. When the show went into rehearsal, Louis Shurr told him, "Buddy, I know a lot of people who'd like to invest in your show." "Doctor," Buddy said, "there's one thing I don't want."

"What's that?" Doc asked.

"I don't want to sit in the Stork Club and have some drunk walk by and say, 'I'm your partner!'" Buddy said. "I've got bonds sitting in the Guaranty Trust Company and I'll use my own dough."

Bert worries and broods more than any six worriers or brooders I've known. The silly part of it is that he has no reason to worry.

157

He's one of the greatest but his worrying reached new heights in *DuBarry*. During rehearsals everybody told him, "Bert, this is going to be tremendous for you," but he kept shaking his head and mumbling, "Ethel's got the good songs. She's got a lot more to do in the show than I have."

After the dress rehearsal, in New Haven, he worried so hard that the next day, when we were supposed to open, he was sick, and we didn't know whether he'd open at the theater or in a New Haven hospital. But he did go on, and there was never a show more evenly divided between two people than that one was between Bert and me. In spite of Bert's stomach churning like a rotisserie, *DuBarry* went over so well on opening night that we came into New York the way we'd opened. Nothing was changed. Bert's every move was right. He could do no wrong He was sensational. But in spite of this, he was still in there worrying, even after we'd knocked Broadway for a goal.

Just before the opening of *DuBarry*, I was tucking away a big dinner when the show's producer, Buddy De Sylva, asked reprovingly, "How can you eat a heavy meal at a time like this?"

Buddy wasn't exactly the phlegmatic type himself; and could be he was shocked at my dragon-lady appetite because he was worrying about Bert's worrying.

"I'm hungry," I told him.

"This is no time for joking," he said sternly.

"Look," I told him, "I may joke about some things, but not about something important like dinner."

When we rehearsed for *DuBarry*, Buddy engaged a dancer to dance with Betty Grable, who made her Broadway debut in the show. The director said to this boy, "When you sing the song, 'Every Day Is a Holiday,' with Miss Grable, hold her hand and look into her eyes as if you're really in love with her."

"I cain't, suh," the dancer said. "I'm in love with a lil' brunette gal in my home town down in Florida, suh. I just cain't do it."

"I want out," Grable said. "What kind of a show is this anyhow? I'm not *that* repulsive."

But she'd signed a contract, she had to open, and a good thing for her too, for she was great. When she came on the audience whistled and cheered and stomped because she was different and fresh. Beauty and fresh talent are things an audience understands. You can't fight them.

I sang, "But in the Morning, No" and "Friendship" with Bert; and "Katie Went to Haiti" and "Do I Love You?"

"But in the Morning, No" together didn't get over too well at first. It was about the things you can do at night, but in the morning you don't feel like doing them. So we hoked it up by giving the impression that we were breaking each other up—which means giving each other uncontrollable giggles and laughter which are not in the book and which look impromptu—but we did them every night the same way and the audience loved it.

No matter how nervous Buddy was about my big dinner before our opening, he wasn't nervous about taking a chance on starring me for the first time. I've mentioned this before. It happened right after *DuBarry Was a Lady*. When I left that show to go into rehearsal for *Panama Hattie*, Buddie put my name over the title alone: ETHEL MERMAN IN PANAMA HATTIE. When he told me what he was going to do, I went out and looked at the marquee, and I said to myself, *Just look at that, will you!* Then I turned and eyed the passers-by and tried to send them a thought wave that said, "Get a load, everybody. It's me, it's me, it's me!"

As musical comedy plots go, *Panama Hattie* had heart; but recently, when it was translated into a television show, it didn't work out well. It was cleaned up so much—which meant leaving out some of its best songs—that it might as well have been called *Elsie Dinsmore in the Canal Zone*, for all the moxie it had. Also, it was condensed until it resembled evaporated milk. But it ran fourteen months on the stage—from October 30, 1940, to December 27, 1941, so it couldn't have been too feeble in that version.

In it Jimmy Dunn was my love interest. He had a small stage daughter played by Joan Carroll. I met them in Panama. I forget why they were there, but before meeting Jimmy and his child I knew nothing about etiquette and proper dressing. I was always hanging around with sailors, done up in an orchid-colored dress, tricked up with bows, doodads, and gewgaws. In short, I was pretty much of a floozy. The small successor to Shirley Temple who was the offspring of my boy friend taught me better.

The scene when little Joan showed me how to be a lady was cute. She made me take off the bows. The audience thought she was snipping them off with scissors, but they were just snapped on, so it only looked like she was cutting them. When the little tot had me all cleaned up, combed and groomed, I latched onto her daddy and we lived happily ever after.

There was a tenderness in the duet, "Let's Be Buddies," I sang with the little girl. Sometimes it even jerked tears from

160

strong, gruff silent men in the audience. I never saw so many executives, bankers, and brokers blowing their noses and taking cinders out of their eyes with handkerchiefs.

Rags Ragland, Pat Harrington, and Frankie Hyers played three sailors in *Panama Hattie*. They ripped and roared, they ogled the girls, they sang lyrics that were barely printable. I loved Rags. Once, when he was being interviewed, he described the difference between burlesque and Broadway like this: "On the burlesque stage you've got to get out there and punch for your laughs, but Broadway audiences are primed and ready to laugh the minute you step out of the wings." Then he thought of another difference. "Broadway audiences wear ties too."

Chapter Twelve

It was when I was in *Panama Hattie* that I met my second husband, Bob Levitt, a newspaperman. I'd been married before, for less than a week, to a man named Bill Smith—I mean I'd only worked at it that long. It was such a failure and it was over so quickly it almost seemed something that never happened. For a fan-mag story I'd skip the next few paragraphs, but since this is the story of my life, with me holding back only those things which might hurt someone, here goes: Mr. Smith passed through my life briefly. We lived together about three days. In those three days he knew it was wrong and I knew it was wrong. I married him in an impulsive moment. I take it that he did the same.

When I met Smith, he was an actor's agent with the Charlie Feldman agency in Hollywood. I met him in New York; then he went back to California. There were lots of long-distance calls and much *amour* over the phone. He said, "Let's get married," so we were married one Friday in Elkton, Maryland.

It was among the shortest honeymoons on record. Smith had to go back to the Coast the following Sunday. His job was on the Coast and I was in New York in *Panama Hattie*. We thought it over and called it quits. A Mexican divorce let us out of our trap. That's all. I'm this kind of a dame: when I'm finished with something, I write period at the end of it. I never leave anything hanging in air. The same goes for people too.

But to get back to *Panama Hattie* and Bob Levitt, I found out that he hadn't seen me in it, although he'd begun to beau me around. When I made some reference to the past shows I'd been in, he gave an evasive answer. Finally I asked him about a particular show of mine. He admitted he hadn't seen it. I ran through all my shows. I found that he'd never seen me on the stage.

I looked him in the eye and I said, "A fine beau you are. There'll be two tickets at the box office tomorrow night in your name. Use them or don't bother to come around to see me any more."

Levitt took a newspaper friend, Sterling North, with him to see the show, and he had quite a few drinks beforehand, to brace him for the ordeal. Sterling told me later that my swain had a hard time staying awake to watch me.

"It bored the hell out of me," Levitt said afterward. "I never particularly liked musical comedy, although it appeals to some people." Most people find it hard to go to sleep while I'm singing but it wasn't that way with unentranced Levitt. Well, thank God musical shows appeal to *most* people.

At first our courtship was complicated because each of us thought that the other wanted to stay up nights. As a result neither of us said, "For goodness' sake, let's go home," when we got sleepy. This was bad because we had a problem getting our work hours to blend. Levitt had a day job and I had a night job. When I was through with my show at night, I wanted to go for a sandwich or something, and maybe he had a meeting coming up in the morning, and he'd been working all day and he was tired anyhow.

Finally we worked out a system. I'd have my dinner at home at six, before going to the theater. Levitt would go home from his work and lie down and have two or three hours' sleep while I was on the stage. Then, if I wanted to go out after my show, he'd come down to the theater and pick me up and out we'd go. That way it wouldn't be so tough on him because, even if he had to get up at eight the next morning, he'd have put in a fortifying three hours of sleep.

When we were married in Connecticut, he was making upwards of two hundred dollars a week as promotion director of the *Journal-American*. That was a fat sum by newspaper standards in those days, but by show-business standards it wasn't such a much. However, how much Levitt and I made didn't enter into things with me although maybe it did with him. I can't see why the man feels he has to carry an equal amount of the financial burden or more. The average man—even a successful one—can't afford to run a big house and keep me in fancy clothes and jewelry too. I don't think it's his business to do it. If I want those things, I ought to pay for them myself.

I was lucky enough to earn respectable sums of money in the pre-high-tax days. I salted most of it away in trust funds for myself and my children. I've noticed that people don't like to think that the entertainers they've been fond of are broke. I know that whenever I hear the names of some of my old favorites I find myself hoping they still have some of the do-re-mi they've made. It's sad but a lot of people who were big earners haven't saved very much.

Nowadays, taxes being what they are, even if you make a big salary it's tough to keep it, but I've always made it a rule to live on the same scale when I'm making a lot as when I'm not making it. Show or no show, none of that big, splashy stuff like keeping a bevy of French personal maids for me. I did buy some jewelry, but that was more of an investment than self-indulgence.

Not that I've been a killjoy. Most of the actors who've worked with me remember me sticking my head out of my dressing room and yelling happily, "Let's get a big black car and go somewhere!" It was one of my favorite sayings. However, it was just an expression. After the show, if we went to a cabaret, we didn't need a big black car; we could take a cab or we could walk.

I do bookkeeping on my expenses. Formerly, when I was on a trip, I set down each item of expense in a little black book even if it was only a magazine, a stamp, or my contribution toward the upkeep of a powder room. I don't have to do much of that any more because, when I go out to the Coast to make a movie, or to New York to be in television, I put such things on the hotel bill. That way the hotel keeps my petty-purchases accounts for me.

But I keep on top of the budget for the household expenses each week just the same. I've got a governess-housekeeper who does the shopping. I give her the money to go to market. When she comes back she gives me the list of things she's bought and the bills and I write it down in a book and keep track of it all. In that way I know what's spent each day. At the end of the week I have an idea of what it's cost to run the house that week. If it's not within a certain figure, something's wrong, and maybe I should return a couple of empty bottles and get the deposit back to balance things up.

The trouble with my hiring domestic help is this: the moment the applicant hears my name and realizes who I am, she begins to be afraid of late parties. This was especially true when Broadway was my workbench. But the truth was, it was just the opposite. I had no late parties. I had to have dinner at six, so I could relax before the show, and I liked to eat dinner with my feet propped up. The doctor said it was good for me. And I had to put up my hair in bobby pins. Half the time I'd eat alone, from a tray in my room. Moreover, I wasn't much of a cocktail-party-goer. I didn't have the time and I didn't want to waste my energy.

I brought prospective servants over to the apartment and showed them through it. If I hired them, sometimes they stayed fifteen minutes and sometimes as long as two or three days. After watching them whip in and whip out, I told my husband, Bob

Levitt, "Maybe you'd better put a revolving door in here to handle this traffic."

They were frightened before they were hurt. Any time we gave a party, like a cocktail party on a Sunday afternoon, I employed caterers. The work wasn't hard, but they didn't wait for the late parties they were sure I'd throw before they claimed that they were tuckered out.

Whether I'm a good housekeeper or not, a lot of people were convinced that I wouldn't make a good mother. There were broad hints by various broads that I wasn't the maternal type. Well, since I have been a mother, I've noticed that those same people now accuse me of being too devoted and too indulgent. I ask you: can you win? I try to treat my children like people instead of imbeciles. I guess it's this that led up to a conversation I had with little Ethel several years ago on Thanksgiving when she wouldn't eat her food. "Listen, Little Bit," I said, "if you don't eat that turkey I'm going to eat you."

Little Bit was interested as all get out. "Then I'll be right back in your tummy again, won't I?" she asked.

I don't remember what I said. Nothing very clever, I'll bet. I'd told her the facts of life when she was six; anyhow when she was old enough to understand. I wanted to tell her myself rather than have somebody else tell her in a messy way.

Every time people came to see us, I invited them up to the nursery to see our kids, and when I left the house I carried a wallet in my handbag. In it was one of those sections of cellophane envelopes that hold snapshots. I had shots of our kids sitting down, standing, on the potty, off the potty. If people were slow about getting into a bright-saying-of-kids contest, I opened the wallet and flashed Little Bit and Little Bobby at them. I don't carry those snapshots now, but wherever I go I lug a picture of the two of them to keep on my dresser.

I'm proud of the fact that my children talk to me as easily as they talk to friends their own age. When I go out with Little Ethel, it's like being with a girl friend. She's only twelve, but she's just great. For that matter, I've never talked to either of my kids as if they were babies. I try not to use profanity when they're around, otherwise I pull no punches with them. If they need a bawling out, they get it. I give it to Ethel with a woman-to-woman approach, and with Little Bobby, woman-to-man. I sit down and reason things out with them. Sometimes they even see it my way when I'm through.

Little Ethel pulls no punches either. A few years ago she came to a rehearsal of *Call Me Madam*. On the way she said, "Mom, would you stop by the newsstand and buy me some comic books?"

"Sure," I said, "but you're coming in to watch a rehearsal and I don't want to look out into the theater and see you reading comic books."

I compromised on getting her some comic books "to read later." What she meant by later and I meant by later were two different things. I don't think she took her nose out of those books while she was in the theater. There I was, trying to remember lines, and looking down and seeing Little Ethel in the second row with her head in a comic book. If they ever start to give out comic books instead of programs to grownups in theaters, that's it, brother!

Afterward someone asked me, "Why do you suppose she came in the first place?"

That's easy. I'd asked her to come and she didn't want to hurt my feelings.

As far as our kids were concerned, Levitt and I—and now Six and I—agreed that certain things should be done about them and we stuck to it pretty well. We had a strict policy about not letting the kids participate in my career. I don't use them to pose for pictures or junk like that. We had a very strong feeling that it wasn't fair to the children to handicap them with that kind of notoriety, because, after all, they have to go to school with kids who will not take kindly to their identification with a star.

There was one thing I couldn't do with my kids. When I was in a show—which was most of the time—I couldn't have dinner with them every night, because they ate before I did. They had their dinner about five-thirty. I ate around six-fifteen or six-thirty. They had their big meal in the middle of the day and a light supper at five-thirty, so eating with them would have made things too complicated.

I've always been crazy about kids—anybody's kids. I have no sense of proportion about them. If anything happens to mine, I go to pieces. I can face a crowd in the biggest theater and it doesn't bother me, but if anything happens to my children, I can't take it.

I'll give one example to show what I mean. When Little Bobby was three and had just learned to walk—this was when I was liv-

ing with Levitt at 25 Central Park West in a duplex apartment—
I was downstairs in the foyer, and I saw Little Bobby walking
behind the railing on the landing, on his way to the top of the
staircase. He had on his pajamas and bathrobe, but his bathrobe
wasn't tied and he tripped over the unknotted sash.

I saw him go bump-bump-bumping downward, and instead of
picking him up, I ran blindly the other way, to get away from
what I'd seen. I rushed into the servants' dining room, sat on a
chair, and had myself a big fat case of hysterics. Even with my
eyes closed I could still see that little figure tumbling and tumbling. The sight was burned on my eyeballs. Luckily, he was such
a fat roly-poly he wasn't really hurt, only scared and bruised.

I don't know why it is. I have plenty of guts when it comes to
anything else; I can stand pain and it makes no difference, but
when it comes to kids I fold.

The apartment in which I lived with Levitt at 25 Central Park
West had a two-pool terrace; or at least that's what we called it.
The terrace was tremendous and was shaped like a capital L. I
read somewhere that it was an acre big. I don't think it was that
large, but it might have been a half acre. The part of the terrace
on the Sixty-second Street side was 125 feet long. Then it made a
right turn and became a roof garden. When we first moved in we
had goldfish in the rock-garden pool. We also had a wading pool
built and enclosed by a brick wall. The children waded there summers.

The view was terrif! From one side I could see all Central Park.
And I could look right down Broadway. From the Sixty-second
Street side we could see the *Queen Mary* and the *Elizabeth* dock-

ing and going out. The kids got a jar out of that. Did I say "the kids"? I know a couple of older kids who got a jar out of it too.

Against the east wall of the living room in my New York apartment was a bookcase. Among other books it held *Sanctuary*, *Nana*, something by Strindberg, and a *Business Arithmetic*. These were just props. I never read a line of any of them—except the arithmetic, which was a hangover from my secretarial days.

I was supposed to have one of the best collections of perfume in town. I doted on one called Tailspin. I use the past tense because I don't think they make it any longer, or maybe they call it Shack-Up No. 5 now. Anyhow, it wasn't too strong. It had a sort of flowery fragrance to it. I used to have a mirrored top to my dressing table and I got a big kick out of seeing fancy perfume bottles all around. But along with other changes that have been made, I don't use perfume any more. I just use eau de cologne. How you say eet een deese country? More genteel!

Thinking of Levitt and our life in New York makes me think of still another Duke of Windsor story. We had been asked to go to a party that Mrs. Hearst was giving for the Duke and Duchess. We were to drop in after the theater.

I went to the theater and Levitt and my picture agent, George Rosenberg, went on to the party. I met them there about 12:30 A.M. It was a big, big soiree; everybody who was anybody in New York was on deck in their fanciest. We weren't familiar with everybody by any means, but Mrs. Hearst came up and grabbed me and was very nice and friendly to Levitt and George.

We noticed that there was this little table set up in the center of the living room and the Duke and Duchess were sitting there.

I'd met the Duke before but Bill Hearst was trying to introduce Levitt and George to the Duke and Duchess. He said, "Eddie, my friend, I want you to meet Bob Levitt and George Rosenberg." Then his mind took a trip off someplace and he said, "Bob and George, I want you to meet Eddie England!"

I can't explain it, but while I laughed at Bill Hearst's blooper at the time, I found the name he gave the Duke kind of touching when I looked back on it. I mean, after all, there was a time when he *had* been Eddie England.

Levitt always claimed the theory a lot of people had that I was a Broadway baby was wrong. He said it gave only a superficial picture of me. His claim was that I regarded my career as a business, like a man going to his office, and that when I was through with it for the day or for the night I was through. He was right. I did my job the way I did when I was a stenographer. When I closed my dressing-room door—wherever it happened to be—that was it.

Now that I'm living in Denver, people are always telling me how much I must miss New York and how much I must miss being in a Broadway show. I tell those people that I'm happy doing what I'm doing, which is being a wife, a mother, a housekeeper, and a part-time movie and TV performer, and if they don't believe it just look at me. That ought to prove it.

I bring this up in case anybody remembers an article I once wrote for *Cosmopolitan* magazine. Bob Levitt helped me write it and the editor said it was quite amusing. It was all about my not wanting to leave the signs that flash on and off all night in order to travel out into the country for a weekend. In that piece I said that I hated to leave New York even overnight. I said I could see no good reason to leave the building in New York at 25 Central Park West, where I lived, and go someplace else.

I'd moved into it in 1933, with Mom and Pop. We'd taken an apartment on the tenth floor. Then we'd moved to the seventeenth floor, where there was a terrace. When I married Levitt we took an apartment on the twenty-first floor of the same building. I love the sun, so that was ideal. All I had to do Sunday mornings was get up and get out on my own tarpaper beach and I'd have a gorgeous coat of tan all summer long. I even overheard people say, "She must have a place in one of the Hamptons."

I liked my Central Park West address. While I lived there I was only eight minutes away from the theater district.

As for those who owned or rented a little colonial stone or stucco jobby out in the country, I asked, What's the point of having a house in Far Harkaway or East Jeeterville and such popular haymows unless you have guests to share your solitude and your spool beds and your quaint bathrooms and your quaint maid of all work? So you have guests. That means that you work all day seeing to it that they're taken care of and kept supplied with drinks, and come Sunday night that they're given a big buffet supper. I said that I was all for letting my friends take those little houses—not me. Occasionally, if I was talked into going, I went, but those nests on a country lane at the end of a toll road were for the birds.

Most Sundays I took it easy, stayed home, and rested. I didn't even get dressed. I'd put on a pair of pajamas, or a negligee, or a bathing suit, loll around, have a nice dinner, and listen to the

173

radio or, after TV came in, I'd watch the TV shows. Saturday nights after the show I'd go to a party or whatever was cooking. But no weekend trips! No, sirree! I even hated to go up the Boston Post Road to Rye and Mamaroneck. As for the Pennsylvania countryside, that was early American Siberia with hex signs.

That, my friends, was pretty much how I felt when I lived high above Central Park. Now that I'm living in Cherry Hills, an attractive and beautiful suburb of Denver, my ideas have changed. To use a phrase I heard someplace, "How it looks all depends on where you're sitting."

I've gone back to New York only a few times since I moved to Denver, but each time I do I get a feeling that things have speeded up crazily since I left. We don't hit that kind of pace in Denver. When I go back to New York now, I'm out every night for dinner, and making the spots afterward—the Stork, Morocco, 21, Lüchow's—it's the old routine, except more of it and I am glad to get home to Denver where I can hit the sack at a reasonable hour.

Nowadays, when I'm in New York, it takes me several nights to gear myself up to it, and by the time I've made it I'm bushed. I actually heard myself ask, not long ago, "I wonder how New York people stand it?"

During her babyhood, Little Ethel was called Little Bit. Her father gave her that nickname. Eventually she decided that she wanted to be called Ethel. After that, the only one who could call her Little Bit was her father. Levitt used to say that she was a miniature version of me. When she was very small and I was working in a Saturday matinee, he'd take her to lunch. Afterward he'd tell me, "Taking her on a date is like taking you out, except she's five. She talks the way you do, she walks the way you do, she even yells at me the way you do."

When I was playing *Annie Get Your Gun* in Boston, Levitt brought Little Bit to a matinee. She was four then, and they sat in the first row. Little Bit is a great lover of birds—in fact, of all living things, large or small, bugs to horses. And when her father brought her to see *Annie Get Your Gun* and she watched me shoot the stuffed bird off a lady's hat, she wept aloud. I remember seeing her going up the aisle wailing, "I want to go home!" That's the last I saw of her until after the show.

A newspaper writer reported that after watching me shoot the stuffed bird, she said, "Brother, that's all!" and could not be persuaded to return. The truth is she said nothing of the kind. After all, she was only four. Levitt took her back to the Ritz-Carlton, where she was staying with my mom.

When I got back home, I asked her, "Why did you want to go home?"

"You were killing that bird, Mommy," she said. "You were shooting it."

"But, Little Bit," I said, "it was just make-believe. I wasn't killing a real bird." I don't know whether she believed me or not.

More than one columnist made use of the fact that my relations with Little Bit resembled those of a couple of girl roommates. But it's not true that she ever said to someone else, when I was singing at a party, "Let's get out of this. It's too noisy in here."

There's a famous anecdote concerning a conversation I'm supposed to have had with Little Ethel in Central Park. I'm supposed

175

to have asked her if she wanted to take a walk, and she said, "No." I asked her if she wanted to have a soda, and she said, "No." Finally I was supposed to have asked her, "Do you want to go to the zoo?" and when she said, "No," I asked, "Well, what the hell *do* you want to do?"

The only thing wrong with this is that it didn't happen. I'm no nice Nelly, but profanity is out so far as my kids are concerned. I weigh every word I say in front of them.

But there's one true story about them I'd like to tell. Levitt and I had a pew in St. Bartholomew's in New York, and we used to go there every Sunday morning. When our children were young and first started going to Sunday school, they attended late Sunday school, which began at eleven o'clock. As they grew older, Little Ethel began to catch the nine-thirty morning Sunday school, but Bobby was still on the eleven o'clock kick. One Sunday morning when we were driving to St. Bartholomew's in a taxi, Bobby asked, "Big Bob and Mom, where do you sit when you go to church?"

"We sit in a pew," Levitt said.

"A pew?" Little Bobby asked.

"Yes," his father said, "a pew."

There was a long puzzled silence; and Little Bob asked, "Does it stink?"

Somehow he'd gotten two kinds of "pew" mixed in his small noggin.

Levitt had a sense of humor that was real pixy and sometimes hard to take, but when I simmered down after one of his jokes I was O.K. Once, when I was between shows, he took me on a trip to California. We went by way of New Orleans; then on to Los Angeles, where I rented a car. Before we left New York, I asked him, "Shall I dig up my driver's license and take it with me?" and he'd said, "You don't need a driver's license in California."

So I didn't take it. He said things like that with such a dead pan that, dumb bunny that I am, I took him seriously.

We were living at the Ambassador in L.A., and when I took the car to shop I did something wrong. I went over a white line which was reserved for pedestrians or something. A policeman came over to me and asked for my driver's license.

"You don't need a driver's license out here," I said, beginning to lose patience with this character who didn't even know his own rules. I didn't have a driver's permit. I had nothing. I didn't even have a slip to prove it was a rented car instead of a stolen car. I remember that because the cop went into that with me.

I also remember saying, "I'm Ethel Merman," and the policeman asking, "Who's that?"

"I sing," I said. "I'm living at the Ambassador with my husband."

"Who said you don't need a driver's license?" he asked, turning a funny color, as if his collar was too tight.

"My husband said so," I said. "I'll call him at the office. He's over at the Los Angeles *Examiner*."

Mentioning the *Examiner* seemed to make a difference, and the officer's color faded a little. I was allowed to put the car in a parking lot, go to a telephone, and call Levitt. He sent somebody over from the *Examiner* and I was squared.

At first I wanted to kill Levitt, but before long it began to seem comical. Especially when I remembered the cop saying, "Oh boy, oh boy, are you going to catch hell when your husband finds out! Oh boy, are you going to get it!"

I didn't catch anything. It was the other way around. I saved a few steaming comments for Levitt—I wasn't too good-natured for *that*—and a day or two later he arranged for the county authorities to make me an honorary sheriff.

If anyone asks me, "Why did you and Bob Levitt break up? Was it incompatibility or a conflict of careers?" I can't honestly answer, except that we both began to be unhappy. We were supposed to be the ideal couple. A month before we split, there was an article about us in a woman's magazine—one of those "their marriage is made in heaven" things.

Levitt has a terrific job, and he's well thought of. For quite a while he was associate publisher of the *American Weekly*. Now he's the publisher. I respect him for his ability as a newspaper executive. I think he has respect for me in the theater, but unfortunately the relations between a husband and a wife are affected by people they know outside of their marriage.

When he was with me, Levitt used to meet stage and screen personalities. Some of them had so much ego and such goofy standards about what's important and what's not that they'd say, "So *this* is your husband!" in a snide way. Levitt was probably smarter than all of them put together, and it may have rubbed the wrong way. Anyhow, it didn't help matters.

Without using names—and it's understandable why I don't—Levitt used to say, "Some of your pals figure that if they're going

178

to entertain an advertiser or a customer and they can produce you at a party it's a lure to some people."

If anyone wants to know whether I'm aware that people have used me as bait from time to time, I am. It begins with a stale gimmick called playing both ends against the middle. The plot is to call somebody up and say, "I want you to come to a party I'm giving for Ethel Merman," then call me up and say, "Ethel, I want you to come to a party I'm giving for old Whosis."

A lot of people have used me as a come-on. Usually, when I've gone to those parties and the shank of the evening comes up, I get up and sing, because—it's a funny thing—but at these parties there's always a piano player on hand. Maybe if I couldn't sing I wouldn't have been invited to parties by some of the people who've asked me but as long as I'm not sure I do my stuff anyhow when I'm asked. You feel different when you know people are taking advantage of you. How do I tell? It's in the air. I can smell it. But by the same token I know other people who would have invited me whether I could sing or not. So it all evens up—at least I keep telling myself that.

One January I was down in Palm Beach, as the house guest of Leon and Carola Mandel of Chicago, and of Mandel Brothers department store there. They'd rented this lovely home in Palm Beach, and I was there for a four-week stay. Bob Levitt wasn't with me because he couldn't get away; he was tied up with his job. My first day there I got a call from an agent who offered me fifteen grand a week if I'd come to Miami and work at a place called Copa City. In spite of the money, I said I wasn't interested. I told the man I was in Palm Beach for a vacation.

Ten days later Eddy Duchin and his wife Chiquita arrived to stay with the Mandels too. At night it was quite a thing because the Mandels entertained lavishly in their lovely home. They'd have a group in for cocktails in the afternoon, and Eddy would sit down at the piano and play and I'd start to sing, because I couldn't resist singing when he played. After the cocktail party the Mandels and their house guests went upstairs and took a nap, had a bath, got into evening clothes, and dropped in at a swank Palm Beach place called El Patio.

About one in the morning Eddy would get up on the bandstand and I'd get up there, too, and sing. Human nature—or at least Merman nature—must be a peculiar thing, for while I wouldn't do that at Copa City for all that money, I was doing it for nothing with Eddy at El Patio because it was fun.

Then from El Patio we'd go to a club on Worth Avenue. Behind this club was a boîte called the Tica Tica. We'd drift in there; there was a piano and the girl singer or whoever they had entertaining would just be sitting around resting her pipes. And Eddy would get up—this would be about three in the morning—and play the piano and I'd sing some more. This sort of thing went on as long as the Duchins were there, which was about two weeks. Leon Mandel was getting write-ups in the Palm Beach paper about how his house guests were practically a road show, and the paper wondered what was going to happen to Leon when his entertaining guests left.

If they'd known what was going to happen to Eddy Duchin when he left, they might not have been so funny about it. Poor soul, when he went back to New York he fell ill and passed away.

But I'm leaping ahead in my story like an adagio dancer. Before this, I took part in an affair called *Something for the Boys*. In that show I was supposed to fall in love with a character named Bill Johnson. I've noticed that for some reason the male lead always has to have one of those all-American names like Johnny Johnson or Bill Jones. Why, I don't know. *Something for the Boys* had a score by Cole Porter, made up of such minor Porter accomplishments as "Something for the Boys" and "He's a Right Guy." The big noise of this opus was an Indian number I sang with Paula Laurence called "By the Mississississississississinewa." It was one of the funniest songs ever written. I wore a weird Indian leather garment, went "Ugh, ugh, ugh," did a stomp, and the people screamed.

Something for the Boys brought me back to the Alvin Theater. It had taken me three minutes to climb the four flights of stairs to my dressing room in the Alvin when I'd had my first big chance there in George Gershwin's *Girl Crazy* in 1930. It had taken me twelve years to get down those stairs to the star's dressing room I occupied in *Something for the Boys*.

After that, a theatrical enterprise called *Sadie Thompson* appeared briefly in my life. I remember calling my old piano-playing pal, Lew Kessler, and asking him if he wanted to work in *Sadie Thompson*. When he said, "Yes," we went to rehearsal together. It was to be a very dramatic thing. When I had the lyrics copied down in my notebook, I asked Lew up to my apartment and we went over them together.

"I don't get any message from these," I told him.

The truth is I didn't understand them. There was a line that went like this: "You put some black pencil on your peepers and some *mal maison* on your lips." I hadn't an idea what *mal maison* was. I knew *mal* meant "bad" and *maison* meant "house," so I figured if you put those two together they meant "bad house," but I couldn't see how you put that on your lips. The lyric writer said it was a brand of lipstick, but I asked fifteen of my girl friends, and they'd never heard of it.

I have to sing songs that make sense to me, and that "*mal maison* on your lips" stuck in my craw. However, I went to rehearsal and they started shooting a lot of dramatic stuff at me about "improvisation" and saying, "Now, try and pretend there's a fly nearing the end of your nose. Imagine that this fly is going zzzzz. Show us how you would act if it lit on your nose."

Since then, I've learned that this is more or less the Stanislobsky (anyway that's the way *I* spell it) method of dramatic training. If it's not Stanislobsky, it's a blood brother to it. They can have both brothers. If a fly lit on my nose, I'd look at it cross-eyed. That would look great from out front, wouldn't it?

I rehearsed for a week. Then I decided I couldn't do any of it—the fly bit or the lyrics. I quit and June Havoc took my place. The show played less than forty performances at the Alvin Theater—*mal maison* on its lips and all.

Chapter Thirteen

Dorothy Fields first had the notion for *Annie Get Your Gun*. She got it in a roundabout way. It was during the war, and Dorothy was at 21 for dinner one night with her husband. Sitting next to the Fieldses was a woman from the Traveler's Aid Bureau at the Pennsylvania Station. That was the spot during the war where the servicemen who came in from Coney Island and Palisades or wherever could stay at the station until their trains left for camp. They'd get coffee, cigarettes, and if they were tight somebody would sober them up and give them a place to lie down.

Dorothy was interested in all this. She was at the Stage Door Canteen three nights a week, so she began to talk about servicemen to this big wheel from the Traveler's Aid. "I had the cutest guy in the other night," the big wheel remarked. "He was a sharpshooter with medals from here to here, and he was tight as a tick. He'd been out to Coney Island and he'd won everything he could possibly win with a gun. Then he'd taken the train to the Pennsy Station and had walked in loaded."

Then, for no reason at all, that Dorothy had a flash; Ethel Merman as Annie Oakley.

She and her brother, Herbie Fields, had a meeting with Dick Rodgers and Oscar Hammerstein the next day to talk it over. It was decided that Jerry Kern would do the music, and Herbert and Dorothy would do the book.

What a combination!

They had nothing on paper. Just nothing. Except they did have an idea for my entrance (the entrance that was afterward used, where you hear a shot off stage and a bird falls off a woman's hat, and you know it's Annie Oakley who's just about to make her entrance). And they had the finish of the first act. They hadn't even discussed story. They planned to stick pretty much to the line of Annie's real life. And the finish of the first act was where her beau, Frank Butler, leaves Annie and she gives the Indian chief, Sitting Bull, Frank's letter to read to her because she's never learned to read.

While the Fieldses were pouring all this out, Dick and Oscar flagged them down and said, "Hey, Ethel's in the hospital. She had a baby only day before yesterday, by Caesarean section. This is very bad, casting her the second day after a Caesarean."

"I'll see her," Dorothy said.

The first I heard of it was when she called me at the hospital and said that she wanted to see me. It was August 13, 1945, two days after my son Bobby was born. Both my babies were Caesareans.

"I have to see you, Mermsy," Dorothy said.

She didn't say what about, so I told her, "I'll call my obstetrician and ask him. After all, I'm in stitches, and not from laughing." Naturally after an operation that serious, there was pain, so I called my obstetrician.

"She may see you for fifteen minutes," he said.

So she went up to Doctors Hospital and said hello to all the nurses on the floor. She knew them very well, having been there herself, and she told them, "I've got to see Mrs. Levitt."

"I don't think you can see her," they said. "She's not very comfortable."

"Tell her Dorothy Fields is here," Dorothy said.

When they let Dorothy in, she asked, "How'd you like to play Annie Oakley? If you'll do it, Dick and Oscar will produce it." Oscar and Dick are not always producers and song writers. Sometimes they are only producers.

"Gee," I said, "I've got gas pains and everything, and here you're talking about me playing Annie Oakley! Let me get out of here. Then I'll let you know."

Dorothy told me later, "Once I had this idea, I went to Oscar Hammerstein and I said, 'What do you think of Ethel Merman as Annie Oakley?' He said, 'Great! We'll tell Dick.' So we told Dick Rodgers, and he and Oscar said, 'We'll do it.'"

The next day it was decided that Jerome Kern, with whom Dorothy had worked for six years, would do the music and she'd do the lyrics, and Herbie—that's Dorothy's brother—and Dorothy would do the book. Dorothy and Herbert had their idea for the opening and a finish for the first act before they even discussed

185

the story with me. It was when they'd gotten that far, Dick and Oscar said, "Maybe you'd better see how Ethel feels about all this." It was then that she'd called me at the hospital.

I recovered fast. In no time I was feeling as sharp as a lady sharpshooter. When they trundled me home I said, "Yes," deals were made, and we went into rehearsal in February 1946.

But to flash back a little, Jerry Kern had come East to do the score. Dorothy had been working with Jerry on the Coast. They'd done several pictures together (among them *Swing Time* for Astaire and Rogers) and they'd won the Academy Award for the song "The Way You Look Tonight." But Jerry'd been out there so long that the thought of a New York show terrified him. He'd come East to do *Very Warm for May*, which was a flop, and he'd said, "I'm not going to go through *that* again."

Oscar and Dick and Dorothy talked to him long distance, and Oscar said, "Look, if we revive *Showboat* and you get back in the theater by way of something you've done and you know it's a success, then you'll get the feel of it again and you'll do *Annie*."

Jerry thought it over. He said at first that he was too old. And he said, "You're crazy." Then he said, "Oh, all right, I'll do it." But before Dorothy and Herbie could start the second act Jerry had a stroke and died.

It was then that Dorothy, Herbie, Dick, and Oscar had a meeting, purpose of the meeting to ask each other: "Who could possibly take Jerry's place?" They kicked this question around for a long time.

Finally Dick said, "The one I think is right for this is Irving Berlin."

"Why didn't you say so before?" Dorothy asked. "Of course he's the *only* person to do it."

Josh Logan had read the first act and had agreed to direct it, and Jo Mielziner had promised to do the scenery. But when Irving was approached he said, "Let me talk it over with my wife Ellin. I'll think about it over the weekend, and if I decide I want to do it at all, I'll read the book. I won't read the book now."

So he talked it over with Ellin over the weekend and he decided to do it. Then he sat down and in eighteen days he wrote ten of the best songs ever written by anybody.

Cole Porter has written some fantastically good songs for me (so did the Gershwins), but it was Irving Berlin's lyrics that made a lady out of me. They showed that I had a softer side. It was about time that I had a softer side, because my hard-boiled Tessie type had become a cliché character. The gangster moll, the hey-hey girl, was good in the twenties and thirties but people didn't care about her any more. She'd gone out.

The right approach today is to make fun of that period and kid it good-naturedly as is being done in New York right now in a production called *The Boy Friend*, and on the *Anything Goes* television show I did a gay twenties doll and she came out fine because we were ribbing the whole thing.

According to Dorothy, Irving was also skeptical about taking on the job because he thought it was out of his line. It called for hillbilly songs, ballads, and fast songs as well as comedy songs —and Irving wasn't sure he had that much variety. I don't have to tell anyone he proved that he had.

187

The whole thing from the first rehearsal to the last performance was a joy.

You never know when Irving is going to get nervous about a song. Sometimes he's right to be nervous and sometimes he's wrong. When we were in Boston breaking in *Annie* he got shaky about "Doin' What Comes Naturally" for some reason. The song was going fine, and Oscar Hammerstein told him, "Why don't you leave it alone?" But Irving thought he could improve it by shortening it. He worked like a dog.

I worked like a dog too, for there's nothing harder than to give a performer *part* of a new lyric to learn, so she has to remember part of the old and part of the new all at the same time. And not only was the song made shorter but there were different lines in Irving's new version. He gave me the new short version on a Tuesday. Then when he came to my dressing room just before the Wednesday matinee, I had his new lyric stuck on the mirror in front of me. I'd typed it out and I was studying it as I slapped on my make-up. That afternoon I sang it letter-perfect.

So guess what? Irving decided that it wasn't as good as the one he'd thought up in the first place. "The audience reaction isn't as good," he said.

If you change a thing, the audience will tell you whether or not you've made a smart move. Even if they applaud, you can tell by the *quality* of their applause—by whether it's thin or full-bodied—how you're doing. We went back to Irving's original lyrics.

Emotionally, my role in *Annie* was stronger than any I'd ever

188

played before. In the opening scene, I was a dowdy doll from Darke County, Ohio; good with a gun, but good with almost nothing else. When I met my man, Frank Butler (played by Ray Middleton), Josh Logan told me, "The first time you lay eyes on Frank, give him a goon look."

A "goon look" was opening my mouth until my jaw dropped almost to my chest, and just standing there struck dumb at the gorgeousness of this hunk of manhood. It went over so well that Josh told me to give Ray that goon look not only that first time I saw him but the next few times as well.

Josh also gave me some wonderful business to do when Ray looked at me and sang "The Girl That I Marry." According to Ray, the girl he married must be as soft and as pink as a nursery, while there I was, in my old flat-bottomed moccasins and my old dirty, flat-bottomed flannel skirt. I had black cotton stockings, and a bunch of quail hanging around my waist, and a whistle around my neck, and I carried a gun. I was bait for catcalls instead of being a whistle stop.

Ray sang to me that the girl he planned to call his own would wear satins and laces and smell of cologne. He'd go on about how her nails would be polished, and how she'd wear a gardenia in her hair, and how, instead of flittin', he'd be sittin' next to her and she'd purr like a kitten. Then he'd walk off, leaving me looking down at myself in despair. I'd finger my dress, and because I was real gone on that man, it was pathetic. Then I'd take my gun, walk across the stage, sit on a bench, and the orchestra started the introduction to "You Can't Get a Man with a Gun."

189

When I was getting ready to relate my story in this book, I asked Josh to tell me frankly how I was to work with, in *Annie*. "You were able to make transitions without asking for cerebral reasons for those transitions," he said.

I've read that over six times and am not quite sure what it means, but whatever it means, I think I ought to have it framed, coming from Josh Logan, because he's one of the theater's really great men.

"In other words," he said, "as an actress you were able to go from high into reverse without the annoying business of going through neutral."

It strained my head trying to figure that out too. I tried to remember a point in a show where I'd gone from high to reverse, and I remembered that goon look. I'd been in high gear just before I'd done that. There'd been a lot of action, with me shooting a bird off a lady's hat, and the shift had been for comedy into an exaggerated love-at-first-sight mugging.

Annie opened in New Haven; then we moved to Boston. It was during one of the evening performances there that I caught my finger in the mechanism of my .22 repeater. I had to pull, aim, and fire. When I pulled, I caught my finger and ripped it open. I wasn't due to make an exit so I had to stay on and sing "Lost in His Arms." Everybody else left the stage, and I tried to hide my hand, which was covered with blood, by playing the scene with the other hand. When I came off, they had the house doctor there and he taped me up.

Most people don't know it, but every theater has a house doctor, the same as a big hotel. There may not always be a doctor in the house, but there's one on call. He may take care of several theaters, but he always has an assistant for emergencies, and the assistant can arrive and go into action by the time they've counted ten over some Thespian who's been decked by sickness or accident.

The assistant they rushed in for me put penicillin ointment on my wound, then, when the curtain went down for the last time, he cleansed it and bandaged it good.

There was a lot of shooting in that show, all blanks, of course, so nobody would get hurt. One of Annie Oakley's biographers has estimated that she must have fired about two million shots in her life, and that she hit something almost every time she fired. In one scene as Annie I rode a motorcycle around the arena on the stage and shot out the lights on the central pole of a circus tent. It was a dark scene and I sat spotlighted, in tights, on a stationary motorcycle with its wheels revolving. The orchestra played hurry music to create the illusion of speed, while I fired a rifle over my shoulder at the turning lights.

During a tryout performance a hot shell dropped on the motorcycle seat. There I was, caught in the glaring footlights, unable to squirm off of it. Instead of being branded by a waffle iron, the way the girl was marked in *Red, Hot and Blue,* I was scorched by a hot shell. I may still have a small scar from that mishap. I'm not sure. It's in a hard place for me to get a look at.

We were just about to open in New York when we just barely avoided a tragedy which could have squashed us all into a pulp. The afternoon before the dress rehearsal we'd been out of the theater only a half hour when a key girder gave way in the flies.

191

All the grids, the big lights, and the scenery came crashing down. The New York opening had to be postponed and we moved to Philadelphia for three weeks while the upper part of the stage was rebuilt.

Little Ethel was pretty skeptical about the show ever opening in New York. I called her from Philadelphia to reassure her. "When Mommy comes home, she's going to stay a long, long while this time," I said.

"You mean if the scenery doesn't break again!" Little Ethel said scornfully. An optimistic child.

I was so smothered in buckskin in *Annie* that I sweated buckets every night. What with the strong footlights and the spotlights and the side lights, I was losing weight like crazy. Not that I minded but it was a damp and sticky way to do it. So I went to the show's management and said that if they wanted me to survive they'd better do something about my one-girl buckskin Turkish bath. "It's a fine way to make my throat close up," I told them, "because I come off in a lather and strip in an air-conditioned dressing room."

I asked if they couldn't have my costume made out of some material that would look like buckskin but wouldn't be buckskin. They found something—I don't know what—but it hung nicely, even to the deep fringe around its bottom, and it was a lot more comfortable.

I got my biggest laugh in *Annie* from the audience when I was making plans to woo Ray Middleton, and I said defiantly, "I'll show him a thing or two. I'll wear my long, low-cut-in-the-front dress!" You never know what will make people fall out of their seats. They didn't fall out of their seats at that crack in the movie version of *Annie* for the simple reason that it wasn't in there.

At the opening of the second act of *Annie,* most of the cast were on deck, since we were coming back to the U.S.A. on a tramp steamer. I was sitting in a deck chair and thinking of Frank Butler and how I'd lost him because I'd been decorated by the kings and queens of Europe and he hadn't, and his male ego couldn't take it. My little brother, Jake Oakley, who was about as big as a pea, was talking to me. Buffalo Bill was on the other side of the deck, and I was mentally off in the sky, thinking about Frank, when I was supposed to see a sea gull overhead, pick up my gun, go "boom! boom!" and the gull was supposed to drop on stage. I was supposed to pick it up, turn to Little Jake, and say, "Take this down to the cook and have him make a sea-gull samitch." Remember I was just an illiterate girl who didn't know how to pronounce "sandwich."

This was a gimmick we'd thought up to rid ourselves of Little Jake because right after that I went into a big scene and before I did it we had to get Little Jake off stage. One night, however, when I went "boom! boom!" nothing came down. Somebody had goofed.

I still had to get rid of Little Jake anyhow so, after waiting a while, I said to him, "Go down to the cook and tell him to make me a sea-gull samitch." No sooner did I have the words out of my mouth than the gull flopped down, and everybody laughed. "What do you know?" I asked. "Apoplexy!"

I don't think it such a bad line.

Another thing: one night during the run of *Annie* some people in the first row brought a bottle of liquor with them. I have no idea who they were. They were pouring booze into paper cups and were sucking away at it, making a lot of noise and disturbing the performance. I was playing a serious scene with Ray Middleton when I made up my mind I couldn't stand it any longer. So I stopped and went downstage on the apron, and I said, "I'd appreciate it if you'd either do your drinking outside or stay here and be quiet."

It was the first time I'd ever done anything like that, but I *had* to. It got a tremendous hand from the rest of the audience, who had a bellyful of those loudmouthed no-goods.

I didn't realize it until I read up on her, but Annie Oakley died as late as 1926. Her husband, Frank Butler, died three weeks later. I thought she'd been back there with Kit Carson or Wild Bill Hickok and those old boys, and that she'd kicked off a long time before she did. Between them, Annie and Frank left a fortune of half a million, quite a bundle for that day, or even for today, for that matter, when a dime buys a nickel's worth— if you don't care what you get for your nickel.

Things like my beef about my buckskin sweatbox I worked out with the management on a reasonable basis, like any problem which confronts grown-up people. There was no temperament. The truth is, temperament gets you nowhere. I blow my stack when something is wrong and I find I've been conned into thinking it's right. But I've seen people flip their lids over nothing. Maybe this means they're trying to seem important to themselves. I wouldn't know.

Whatever they're after, they get nowhere because their reputation for being cranky gets around, and you hear on all sides, "She's awful to work with. Boy! Don't cross her path!"

I believe in asserting myself, but only for things that are important or that will help a show I'm in. In addition to the other things Cole Porter said about me, he once remarked, "I've never seen Ethel angry wrongly."

My philosophy about this shapes up about as follows: any girl who's worth her salt has to fight for her rights once in a while or get shoved around. At one time or another, every star in show business has had to do this. When I was working in *Annie*, one featured player came in wrapped in liquor fumes time after time. It didn't make for a good performance and it wasn't good for the other people in the cast. I took it as long as I could stand it; then went to the Joes who ran things around there and said, "This has got to stop. I work too hard to have my work loused up by a rummy who's getting gassed all the time."

The soak was warned, but it must have taken the form of a gentle pat on the wrist, delivered while the warner was having one or two with the warnee in an Eighth Avenue bar, for the lubricating kept right on; maybe not as badly, but more than anyone could carry and still give a decent performance. One night when this red-nosed reindeer was extra stoned, it was suggested that I get up a petition, have the people in the cast sign it, and submit the offender's name to Equity. Charge: lousing up the show.

I wouldn't do that. If I'd done that, I would have been the one who was labeled bad; I would have been the one who'd put someone out of work. It could be settled easier by a stiff talking-to that went like this: "Look here, you ———, you're going to get the heave-ho if you come in here fried again."

I figured that ought to do the trick. It did.

It was different with someone like my dear pal Rags Ragland, who had a weakness that way. Poor Rags—who's no longer with us—had to have a certain amount of alcohol fueling his spirit lamp to go on the stage. He'd give the same performance whether he'd have five drinks or ten, but if he'd had no drinks at all he lost his fire. As a matter of fact, I don't know why I say that, since I don't remember his ever going on when he didn't have any. I guess it's just a theory of mine. The point is that he could take a few and it didn't hurt his performance.

One of the by-products of *Annie* was a letter from a great American author, John Steinbeck. I've never been a close friend of Steinbeck's, but I'd met him a few times. His letter said:

Dear Ethel:

We seen your show last night and you was wonderful. There were four people from Texas in front of us who explained all the jokes to each other. This was good, because it not only meant that we heard everything twice but understood everything.

I'm keeping that. It'll be something for me to show my grandchildren when Steinbeck knocks off a Nobel prize.

Another by-product of *Annie* was a typewritten notice I pasted up in my dressing room. It said: "General Eisenhower drank here, November 18, 1946." I'd heard he was coming backstage during intermission, and I wanted to have a drink ready for him.

I found out what his favorite tipple was, and I had a highball sent in for him from the nearest restaurant. After he left I didn't rinse his glass. I just left it the way it was, like a high school girl pressing a rose in her memory book.

There're a lot of people who say I'm a tough, armor-plated dame. This is not true. I cry when I'm happy and I cry when I'm unhappy. But I try never to put on a tear-squirting demonstration before anybody. Some people do that for effect. Not little Ethel. If I cry, I have a reason for it and I do it in private.

I've sung some hard-boiled songs in my life and I've acted some hard-boiled roles, but I'm a soft-boiled gal. Last September, when I saw my father off on an airplane at Denver, I stood with my hands against a gate and waited and watched until his plane was out of sight. When you have a father who's pushing seventy, each time you tell him good-by you wonder if you're ever going to see him again.

Pop is absolutely helpless without Mom. I don't know any man who is as dependent upon a woman as my pop is on my mother. He's completely lost without her. I've never seen such a relationship between a man and a woman. When they go away on a trip, he doesn't even know how to start to pack his valise; Mom does that for him. When they go out, she lays out his tie, his shirt, his suit, his socks—everything. And days when he goes to work in the morning, she does the same thing the night before.

She's only his right arm, and I thought, *There is that dear soul taking off for the first time alone in the air,* and I thought of the things that he'd go through alone in New York, completely lost without Mom. On top of that, I had it in my mind that the next day I was going into the hospital for some minor surgery. Pop had insisted that Mom stay in Denver with me until I was out of the sterilized woods. He was willing to make the sacrifice of being alone so Mom could stay with me.

"Do me a favor," he said. "Don't worry about me. I'll be much better off knowing that your mother is with you than if she's home." He's a real sweet guy.

Chapter Fourteen

Annie Get Your Gun ran two years and nine months, or, to be exact, 1147 performances. I'd had a two-year contract in *Annie Get Your Gun*. They wanted me to renew for another season. I was tired. In two years' time I'd had only two weeks off, and playing Annie was a role that made demands upon you. But I said I'd sign for more if they'd let me have six weeks off. They agreed.

At the suggestion of Mr. and Mrs. George Sumers, I took a vacation at Glenwood Springs, Colorado. George is a big wheel's big wheel. He's in oil, he's in rice, he's a successful broker; he has this huge ranch house in Glenwood Springs, more than a hundred miles from Denver; and he's a fabulous host.

Before heading West, I'd gone to a birthday party for Dorothy Stickney. She's Howard Lindsay's wife and she'd played Mother in *Life with Father*. At the party, Dorothy said she and Howard wanted to duck out of New York for a vacation too. They didn't want to go very far and they wanted peace and quiet, which was why they were passing up Europe or places like that. I told Dorothy that I was going out to Glenwood Springs with the children, and if she made up her mind that they wanted to come there, I could promise her complete rest and relaxation. So I got the Lindsays reservations at the Colorado Hotel. I don't think they've ever had a better summer.

There, one day out of the blue, came Howard's idea for me to play Perle Mesta in *Call Me Madam.* Howard was looking out of a window at me when he suddenly yelled, "Hey, I've got a wonderful idea for a show for you!"

"What is it?" I yelled back.

"Perle Mesta!" he yelled.

"Who's Perle Mesta?" I shouted.

"Tell you later," he said.

I wasn't sure who Perle Mesta was. I had to read up on her to find out.

Later Howard said that, when he'd looked down at me, a copy of a weekly magazine with Perle Mesta's picture on it was lying next to me, and he'd said to himself, "Ethel as an ambassadress."

Howard got his writing partner, Buck Crouse, on long distance back in Massachusetts and told him about the idea. Buck thought it great. Then after getting together on long distance they got together in person. The whole thing took about nine or ten months to write. Somewhere along the way they took time out to tell me their story. "This is the way it goes, Ethel," they began. And they told me I was going to play the part of the United States ambassadress to a small mythical European country and how the chargé d'affaires would try to tell me off, and how all the prime minister of that trick little country had to do to turn me into jelly was to look at me.

I could visualize the whole thing, for when Howard and Buck give you a rundown of one of their story ideas they practically act it out. Especially Howard. He prances up and down. He can't talk or even think if he's sitting down.

Howard and Buck lined up Leland Hayward as producer, and Irving Berlin to write the songs. After that, all they needed was a quarter of a million bucks to stage the show. RCA Victor was feeling in an angelic mood. Anyhow, that outfit picked up the tab.

It turned out that Irving was a little short on Mesta knowledge too. When Buck and Howard called him and said, "We've got an idea for Merman as Perle Mesta," Irving said, "I'll have to get my wife to tell me about her."

But after talking to his wife, and reading Buck's and Howard's script, he was very high on the whole thing. In fact he soaked up Mesta's personality so well that once he got a load of it he wrote the perfect Mesta song, "The Hostess with the Mostes'," which was a natural for a woman known for her fabulous party-giving. Sometimes a phrase from a song becomes part of the language and the quotation marks around it get lost. They don't put quotes around "The Hostess with the Mostes'" any more. It just means Perle.

Call Me Madam was the first time I'd asked for and gotten

ten per cent of a show property I was in, as well as a percentage of the gross. I'd been getting ten per cent of the gross before—I'd gotten it in *Annie Get Your Gun*—but I took eight per cent of the gross of *Call Me Madam* and, in addition, I became the owner of ten per cent of the whole property.

I'm the first girl who ever said, "I'm creating the part in this show, so from now on, if any other girl plays the part in another production of the thing, I want a percentage of the take from that production too." My pianist pal, Lew Kessler, was with Joan Blondell when she was in *Call Me Madam* at the State Fair in Dallas and, according to Lew, Joan used to tell him, "Here I am working my head off and that stinker Merman is sitting up there in Denver doing nothing and getting paid for it."

None of us connected with the show were quite sure whether we'd be hung and quartered or shot at sunrise for writing and reciting lines that kidded President Truman. But it's not true that Howard and Buck once got Perle at the legation in Luxembourg on the transoceanic telephone to ask her if it was all right if they did a show about a character who might be mistaken for her. They weren't *that* timid.

Earlier in this story I mentioned that my pal, the columnist Leonard Lyons, arranged a sit-down dinner for me to meet Perle Mesta and Margaret Truman, but I didn't say what happened there. Irving, Howard, and Buck were on hand, and Ezio Pinza and Ray Bolger; it was quite a gathering, but there was a hitch. My son Bobby was running a temperature and I sat with his father, waiting for the doctor to come. I wouldn't leave the apartment until I found out what was wrong. I kept calling Leonard's house and saying, "I'll be there as soon as the doctor comes. He should be here any minute."

When we finally reached the Lyonses', the guests had eaten their way through to the dessert, but Mesta couldn't have been nicer. When I walked in and asked her, "Have you ever had measles?" she understood my problem immediately. She said that if she'd been in my shoes she'd have done exactly the same thing I'd done; meaning that she wouldn't have left the place until the doctor showed.

That was the evening Perle sang "Remember" to Irving Berlin's accompaniment, and I said to Margaret Truman, "If this Perle's going into my racket, I'm going to ask your dad for a job in the diplomatic service."

You'd think a man who's written seven hundred song hits and more in his lifetime, and who chips off a piece of the United States Mint every time he sells a bag of his tunes to Hollywood, wouldn't be a worry wart. If you think that, you don't know our Irving. He practically bit his fingernails to the armpits trying to think up a comedy song for *Call Me Madam*. He kept saying, "I had so many good comedy songs in *Annie*, but I don't have one in this show."

I comforted him by saying, "Maybe a new one wouldn't fit into the story anyhow." Then, in New Haven during the tryout, in just two days' time he wrote the biggest hit of the show, "You're Not Sick, You're Just in Love." I sang it with Russell Nype, and it was a smash. We put it in the opening night in Boston.

The fact of the matter is that, although it was a straight song, what with all the encores Russell Nype and I gave it and the pieces of business we thought up, it worked itself into a comedy song too.

Poor Paul Lukas had to make an entrance after Russell and I had sung the thing. Russell Nype and I would do perhaps two encores of "You're Not Sick, You're Just in Love" in my stage boudoir. Then Paul was supposed to come in, since I had to play a scene with him right after Russell and I were through singing, and the applause subsided. Only Paul wouldn't time it right. He'd walk in and stand there, with the applause swelling up again. There he'd be, in his high-buttoned shoes, and it was very bad for him.

If that happened, Paul just stood there, since it would have looked funny if he'd come on, then backed off again. Finally I worked out a system. I'd make Paul comfortable on a chaise longue and say, "Now you sit there, because we have to do our song again"; I'd prop the pillows up and Russell and I would whip into our ditty once more. Finally I made Paul stand up with us and sing too, although he protested violently, "I can't sing."

That "I can't sing" stuff was an obsession with him, but I said, "Sing anyhow." So reluctantly he took a crack at it.

When it came to singing, his doubts and fears about his singing were so overwhelming that they almost amounted to a phobia. He had so much charm that whether he could warble or not didn't worry anybody else, but Paul brooded about not having a really big singing voice until when it came to singing he froze.

"Don't worry about your singing, Paul," I told him. "Half speak your songs and, what little singing you do, the audience will be agreeably surprised."

At one time when we were in Boston he announced he was quitting the show. "So Mr. Berlin can get someone who can sing," he explained. Paul was so serious about it that a couple of people were actually brought up from New York to audition for his part, but fortunately he decided to stay.

We needed something for the beginning of the second act of *Madam* too, so Irving beat out another song, "Something to Dance About," which took the place of his song, "Mr. Monotony."

During the tryout of *Call Me Madam*, it was obvious to Howard and Buck that one of Irving Berlin's songs, "Mr. Monotony," had no more to do with the plot than a table. Originally it had been in a Metro picture—which picture I don't know—but it had been thrown out of the film only to turn up later in the stage musical *Miss Liberty*. Ejected from *Miss Liberty*, it was then inserted into *Call Me Madam* at the opening of the second act, when I was giving a garden party as a lady ambassador.

Behind me there were two boys and a girl doing a sexy dance, and I'm singing "Mr. Monotony." This is a garden party? It didn't fit, so once more it was given the old heave-ho.

On top of that, Berlin came up with his song, "You're Not Sick, You're Just in Love," which made "Mr. Monotony" look like thirty cents.

Buck Crouse was out in Hollywood in the summer of 1954 while we were readying the film *No Business Like Show Business* and there were rumors that "Mr. Monotony" was going to bob up in this picture. "You know, I think it's actually going to go in this film, Buck," I said. When Buck heard that I thought he'd drop his teeth.

"I hope it is," he said.

"Why?" I asked.

"To get rid of it," he said. "I wish Irving could use it someplace so he could forget it."

In the end they threw it out of *Show Business* but there was talk at Paramount of putting it in Berlin's *White Christmas* at that studio.

But to get back to *Madam*. Howard and Buck both felt that the song was wrong for the show and they made their pitch against it. I didn't say anything. I just went out there and sang it, including the opening night in New Haven. It was no good for me, but I'd kept my mouth closed because I wanted everybody to see how misplaced it was. Then, having given the ditty its chance, I announced: "I've gone along, I've co-operated, I've sung the song, and it doesn't fit. It's out."

A very heavy song, called "Free," was dropped too. The ambassadress fell in love with the prime minister and, not being able to understand why he didn't want a loan for his country from the U.S.A., asked him, "Why don't you go to the people and ask them whether they want the dough? That's why we have elections in our country. That's what freedom's all about."

"We never let the people vote here," the prime minister replied. "They might vote the wrong way."

This was supposed to cue me into Irving's song, "Free," a song that had me up on a soapbox, giving a message to the people that went like this: "Free—the only thing I want on earth is to be free."

The show was *très gai*; the audience liked the love story; they didn't want a thing with a message, so it was decided that "Free" had to go.

Both "Free" and "Mr. Monotony" point up a certain side of Irving—his stubborn, let's-not-waste-anything side. He certainly doesn't believe in throwing things away. He succeeded in getting "Free" into the score of the movie *White Christmas*; only he called it "Snow." He kept the melody but changed the words. And he's determined to get "Mr. Monotony" into something. He'll make it, too. He's very single-minded about such things.

I never dog it about anything in a show. I'm hard-working. I'm professional. I'll try everything anybody wants me to try until I decide it's no good.

Howard and Buck always claim that they don't make any changes in a show after the Thursday night performance of the last out-of-town week—the Thursday night before we open in New York, that is. At least they always said that but they never seemed to stick to it. They always seemed to think of a couple of changes they wanted to make on the Friday before the New York opening and they'd even try to sneak some changes into the Saturday matinee.

A girl has to take a stand somewhere. I remember when *Call Me Madam* was in the last half of its last week in Boston they were trying to sneak in a few more changes. They said brightly, "Tonight we've got a few new little jokes."

I looked them in the eye in a congealed manner and said,

"Boys, as of right now I am Miss Birdseye of 1950. I am frozen. Not a new comma."

Among the members of the cast of *Call Me Madam*, one was an architect, another had been Irving Berlin's office boy, another had been a chiropracter. I didn't know about that last one. I could have used him more than once during the show, when the wear and tear was most wearing and tearing.

Howard and Buck have another story about me that makes them laugh like hyenas when they spring it. It has to do with me going to church in New Haven to take Communion. According to them, I was up there for a tryout, and I wanted to take Communion the Sunday before the show's opening. As I remember it, I went to take Communion all right but somehow I got mixed up on the time and I got to the church an hour early.

Buck and Howard split on what happened next. They both agree that I explained to the priest, "I came here because I want to take Communion. If I'm too early, I can't come back later because I've got a rehearsal."

"Rehearsal for what?" the priest asked.

And I said, "I'm in a show at a theater here this week," so he was nice about it and gave me Communion all alone.

Buck and Howard don't agree as to the pay-off. As Buck tells it, "After he gave her Communion, she told him, 'I'd like to have you come to the theater as my guest. You gave me a show and I'd like to give one for you.'"

Howard says, "It was the other way around. The priest had already seen the show, so he said, 'Well, you gave me a pleasant time so I'll give you Communion right now.'"

Before we say good-by for the moment to those two cutups, Lindsay and Crouse, there's one more story they like to tell about a party at Frank Loesser's at which I sang a duet with Benay Venuta, although we were both pregnant at the time. The second time we stood up to sing, Abe Burrows, who wrote the book for *Guys and Dolls*, said, "We'll now hear from the quartet again."

"It might be a quintet," I said. "How do *you* know what's going on?"

When Perle Mesta came to a matinee of *Call Me Madam*, with Margaret Truman, there was a lot of talk about how everybody connected with the show was worried about Perle's reaction to me obviously playing her. That talk was a lot of malarkey. We thought beforehand that she would take the show exactly the way she did take it—as a lot of fun. Not to horse around with it, I think she was even flattered. It didn't make a bad dame of her.

The way I'd describe the character I played in the show is this: very down-to-earth, but at the same time gracious, a witty character who was also susceptible, warmhearted, and affectionate. She fell in love with her guy in the show as soon as she met him, didn't she?

As for how the Perle in the show matched the real Perle, the real Perle has a certain amount of dignity and class, whereas the footlight ambassadress was brassy and said anything that came into her mind. The real Perle is very intelligent and she can talk on any subject, which I couldn't do in the show. Half the time the stage ambassadress didn't know what she was talking about, but she was likable and lovable, and she pulled a lot of sympathy from the audience. That was particularly true when her prime minister boy friend walked out on her.

Under those wonderful gowns I was a kind of sexy Tugboat Annie gussied up by Mainbocher. The movies always elaborate on things—for instance, in the play I had a wonderful big Mainbocher red lace dress. But in the movie version Irene Sharaff, the designer for Fox, put brilliants on it, which I didn't have on the stage. In the play I wore a very beautiful black and white suit, with a black sweater top and a white skirt and a white cape matching the skirt. In the picture, Irene made a beautiful white coat for me, lined it with red taffeta, and put big black seal cuffs on it. It was to be in Technicolor, and she wanted it to stand out like a sore thumb. It did. In the picture, when I walked along a big corridor carrying a brief case, I saw to it that the coat opened up to show that red lining. And my big, overdone brief case was a camp. "Camp" is slang for something really good; crazy but good, a dilly.

In *Madam* I was properly attired for the first time in my theatrical life. Until then my costumes had never been designed to accentuate any physical charms I may have had as Ethel Merman as opposed to Ethel Merman playing somebody else; if you know what I mean. In *Madam* they were.

The show had been running quite a while before Perle caught it. She chose one of our matinees. She didn't give us any advance notice but someone came backstage during the first act and told us that she was out there with Margaret Truman, Mrs. Truman, and Leonard Lyons.

They didn't come back afterward because, if they had, they'd have been mobbed. But the news leaked out during intermission, and photographers and reporters closed in on them in the lobby. Perle did send me a note, telling me how much she'd enjoyed the show, but I didn't see her again until we played Washington.

However, she did give out an interview in which she compared the two ambassadresses, stage and real. She said, "I only hope that someday I become as great a diplomat as Ethel Merman is an actress." That remark made her about six up on Dean Acheson and Winston Churchill as diplomats.

Chapter Fifteen

For the most part, the gals who've understudied me have had pretty lean pickings, although they've been well paid for waiting for me to come down with something serious and incapacitating.

The kind of outlook a person like me has is this: why should I want anybody to play my part? When you play a part in a play or a musical it becomes a very personal thing to you. It's something you've made yourself. You don't want anybody else dabbling around with it.

The usual fee for understudying me and hoping I'd get laryngitis was six hundred dollars a week. Mary Jane Walsh understudied me in *Annie*, but since then Mary Jane has given up the theater. She lives in East Rochester, New York, now and has a couple of children.

And there's Elaine Stritch, who understudied me in *Madam*. Stritch is a ball of fire. Her glands must go like mad all the time, judging by her energy and drive. The only thing that has ever tired Stritch was waiting to go on. I played a year and eight months in *Madam* and never missed a performance, and Elaine got so sick of inaction that when they revived *Pal Joey* she took a job in it (a speciality in the second act) and understudied me in *Madam—at the same time.*

About eight o'clock she used to pop in on me in my dressing room, eye my healthy condition distastefully, and say, "I gather you're well!"

"I never felt better!" I'd say, and out of the door she'd go.

I think she'd have got sick herself if she hadn't had something to do. However, when *Madam* went on the road, she played my role for a year. She was very good at it.

Understudies have to audition for their roles just like principals. When the understudy just before Stritch gave notice that she was leaving, Stritch did four auditions before she was hired. She got the job in June. This meant that she had to stay in New York for three months in the summer, but hers wasn't a bad job. She rehearsed six hours a week. Evenings she didn't have to come to the theater if she didn't feel like it. She could call in at eight o'clock and say, "If you want me, I'm at the Stork Club," or "I'm at such-and-such a place. I can be reached here from eight-forty till eleven."

This had been going on for some time when Jule Styne, a songwriter-producer pal of Stritch's, called her and said, "I've a part for you in the revival of *Pal Joey*. It's small, but good. We're not going on the road. We're opening cold in New York."

Stritch asked herself, *Why can't I keep on understudying Mer-*

man, be in Pal Joey, too, and draw two pay checks a week? Anyhow, no harm in trying.

So she went to see Jule and said, "I'd like to do *Pal Joey* in the worst way, but I'm understudying Merman. Will you give me your word that if anything happens to Merman I can still replace her and my own *Pal Joey* understudy can go on for me?"

When Jule said, "Yes," she went to Leland Hayward, who was producing *Madam*, explained the deal to him, and he agreed. But when the Equity spokesman heard of it he asked, "What's this? A woman with two jobs? Wait just a minute!"

But since it had never happened before there wasn't any precedent that made it unlawful, so Stritch was home free. Then complications began to set in. Two days before *Pal Joey* was to open in New York, Dick Rodgers cased the production and announced, "It needs a lot of refurbishing and tightening up, so we'll go up to New Haven for five days while it's done. We'll open Christmas night in New Haven."

You can imagine how Stritch felt, since her *Call Me Madam* job meant she had to be on call in New York. But Stritch is a very determined girl. *There must be a way out of this*, she thought. *New Haven is only an hour-and-a-half drive by auto. I can get in my car and make New Haven by ten, after checking at eight with Merman*. She didn't go on in *Pal Joey* until after ten o'clock, which fitted into the schedule she was planning.

However, when *Pal Joey* opened on Christmas night, she had to take the train to New Haven because there was a blizzard, so she said to Leland Hayward, "This once, can I please check with

Merman at her home tonight at seven-thirty, so I can take a seven-thirty-five train to New Haven?"

"Yes," he said. "This one night I'll give you leeway."

She checked with me by phone, I said, "Fine," and Stritch boarded the train. But on account of the blizzard the train didn't leave the station until eight-ten. *This cooks it*, she thought, *because I'm due on stage at ten-thirty.*

When she reached New Haven the clock hands said ten sharp; there were thousands of people waiting for cabs, and there were no cabs. She had a Christian Dior suit on, so she was dressed for her part. She'd bought make-up at the Astor drugstore in New York and had used it on the train, so she was ready to go. She got off the train, ran out in front of the station, opened a car door —the first one she saw—hopped in, and said, "Take me to the Shubert Theater."

The car happened to be full of foreigners, but fortunately they spoke English—or at least they understood the word "Shubert." There were eight—five in back, three in front—and they were startled when they saw Stritch loom up, but they took her to the theater. When she walked in, her understudy was all suited up on the side lines, waiting for the kickoff, but Stritch took off her snow boots, put on shoes, and walked out on that stage. She was so happy to be there that she gave the best performance of her career.

During the five days of the New Haven workout she kept up a man-killing schedule. She'd go to the theater in New York, ask me, "Are you all right?" and I'd say, "Swell." She'd leave the

215

theater, drive to New Haven, do *Pal Joey*, drive back to New York, go to bed, get up the next day, and do it all over again.

Matinee days were fantastic. She'd get up in New York, check with me at two o'clock in the afternoon, drive to New Haven, do a matinee of *Pal Joey*, drive back to New York, check with me for the night show at eight, drive back to New Haven, do the night show; then drive back to New York. Then she'd go to bed. Who wouldn't have gone to bed? Even Gargantua would have sacked in.

A nice Yale-graduate boy for whom she'd done a show at the Yale Dramatic Association did some of her chauffeuring for her. That helped, but until *Pal Joey* opened in New York she spent a large part of five days on the Merritt Parkway.

Stritch told me one story about an old frump who was up to her blue-rinsed hair in the Social Register. It just killed Stritch when she told me about this old harridan. She got hysterical, gasped for breath, and slapped her thighs. It seemed that after one of her performances during the road-company tour of *Call Me Madam* this socialite bag came up to her and said, "I want you to know that I like you much better than Ethel Merman in this thing. You know why? You look more like Perle than Ethel does."

Stritch is a handsome blond wench, five feet eight or nine, with luscious curves yet; and while Perle is kind and generous, and has more personality than anybody, and hundreds of people love her, nobody claims she's a sexy blonde.

When the National Company tour of *Call Me Madam* reached Los Angeles, Stritch checked in at the Beverly Hills Hotel. She was making a study of how to hold her notes for long periods of time and she was being very serious and intense about exercising her pipes. In the morning about eleven or twelve she'd go out into the patio that was connected with her room and vocalize. She was also going in for developing deep notes, like an Italian opera singer. While she was vocalizing and screaming her phone rang, and a voice said, "Miss Stritch, I'm awfully sorry but this is the Beverly Hills Hotel management and we're asking you to give up your room."

"What's the matter?" Stritch asked. "What have I done?"

"You're living next to a woman who likes quiet; she can't stand the noise," the voice said.

Stritch took it big. "It's one o'clock," she said, "everybody's up, no one's sleeping, and I'm a singer who has to get ready for a show tonight."

"I'm sorry," the voice said, "but she's a very important woman and she just can't stand it any longer."

Stritch can take a lot and make like Little Nell but if you keep on riding her she comes on very strong, so she got mad and asked, "Who is this woman who can't stand my noise? You hold the phone and I'll go and have a talk with this woman who can't stand my vocalizing."

"She's in 104," the voice said, so Stritch went out into the hall and whanged on 104. The "important and sensitive" dame opened the door. It was me. The picture version of *Call Me Madam* was about to start, I'd checked into the hotel myself, and hearing Elaine's unmistakable voice, I'd wanted to say, "Hi," to her.

That same summer Dorothy Fields checked in at the Beverly Hills Hotel too. I had rooms just around the corner from Dorothy so, what with Stritch and Dorothy both being there, it was just like Girls' Town.

My onetime understudy, Mary Jane Walsh, has a big sock voice, but not going on night after night was the story of her life too. She spent years waiting for my vocal cords to fray more than temporarily but no dice; although she did go on a couple of times when I had a bad cold. Once, during one of these times, when Mary Jane was replacing me, she was riding in a taxi with her fiancé, Ernie Holtz, a band leader who had a band at El Morocco, and he had a sudden heart attack and died. Mary Jane faced the problem: Should she go on for me anyhow? She decided Ernie would have liked it that way, and went on, although she collapsed right after the performance.

And I've had other substitutes. There was Betty Garrett and Vivian Vance. Vivian is now part of the cast of the TV hit, *I Love Lucy*. The producer of my show—whoever he was—used to try to arrange it so that the understudy had a part in the show too. For instance, Betty Garrett had a part in *Something for the Boys*.

I even had replacements for gowns. A replacement for one gown I wore in *Madam* ran between $1500 and $1750. During the run of *Madam* a reviewer commented: "From inside eleven thousand dollars' worth of Mainbocher draperies, the voice of Ethel Merman cannonaded the far walls of the Imperial Theater Thursday night for the 3923rd time." He might have been right about the 3923rd time, but a lot more than $11,000 worth of clothes by Mainbocher were wrapped around me in that show. One of my gowns was a beautiful red number which required yards and yards of lace. It went on and on and on; but in spite of its beauty it took quite a beating. I also wore bracelets, and the rhinestones in the bracelets caught in the lace. The resultant damage couldn't be fixed by sewing, and I used up three of those red lace dresses during the New York run.

In *Call Me Madam* I also wore a silver lamé court dress that required as much handling as the Super Chief. Anyhow, it seemed as long as the Super Chief, and I was always kicking its observation car out of my way. When we went to Washington for a four-week engagement, Leland Hayward had an entire new wardrobe made for me, and when I left the show in Washington he made me a present of all those dresses. People tell you that Hayward is a big man. I can tell you *how* big.

I wore that red lace dress a lot in private life. When the show closed, I went out to Denver for a party. I wanted to wear this dress there, so I had it shipped to Colorado by air freight, in a big box. The shipping charges came to thirty bucks. A dress like that is good and bad too. It's bad because, once you've worn it, everybody's seen it and they won't forget it, and if you wear it a second time they say, "Here she comes in that red lace dress again." The more spectacular the dress, the shorter its life. This one was so spectacular, its life was shorter than a fruit fly's.

For the tryout of *Madam* they shipped my dresses from New York to New Haven, and from New Haven to Boston, and from

Boston back to New York, in huge, specially made wooden crates. Those crates were so big they were sent by truck or Railway Express.

Talking about my wardrobe for *Madam*, I remember a two-sentence sparring match I had with Mainbocher when he was running up twelve or fifteen thousand dollars' worth of frocks for me. He looked at my head critically and asked, "What are you going to do with your hair?"

I could have said, "Look, bud, you stick to your pins and needles and scissors, and I'll take care of the stuff above my neck." I didn't. I was a lady. "I'm going to wash it," I said. After that he stuck to dresses.

Chapter Sixteen

I won't forget October 20, 1951, in a hurry. On that date Leland Hayward, the producer of *Call Me Madam*, invited the whole cast of the show to a "first-anniversary party." It was given upstairs in the Blessed Event Room at the Stork Club. The Blessed Event is a big room for private parties, but that's not the reason why I'll remember it. I was supposed to go with a friend named Charlie Cushing. But Charlie was playing in a golf tournament the next morning; he knew the Hayward shindig would keep him up late, and it was an important golf tournament. So I went with Milton Holden, a friend of Charlie's. Milton's nickname is Doc, although he's not a medic; he's a broker. While I was having dinner, between the matinee and the evening performance, I got a call from Doc. He wanted to know if it would be all right if he brought some extra people along.

I knew it was going to be a buffet affair, and five or six more would make no difference at a gathering of four hundred people. So I said, "Why not?"

When Doc picked me up, after the Saturday-night performance of *Madam,* he had five or six other people with him. Among them was a big Coloradan named Bob Six. I'd never seen him before, but I thought, *He's nice;* and I envied his date for the evening.

Leland had reserved a huge table for me at the party, but when we were seated, I found myself sitting next to the man who'd brung me. It seemed a Mid-Victorian fate but I figured that one out in jig time. I was the star of the show, wasn't I? It was up to me to do a lot of mixing, wasn't it? So I got up and began to table-hop. By a strange coincidence, when I came back I found myself seated next to Mr. Six, and we started a conversation.

I listened to him and looked him over closely. He is tall, handsome, and muscular. In short, he's a doll. Later I discovered that he had been coming to New York about once a month. His business brought him there that often, but he'd never bumped into me. And I'd never bumped into him. Since then we've discussed how strange that was.

When we got up to dance I asked, "Do you live in New York?" He said, "No."

"Where do you live?" I wanted to know.

"Denver," he told me.

Denver, I thought. *H'm'm'm. Gold miners.*

"I know Colorado," I said. "At least I know Glenwood Springs. I've vacationed there."

"I'm acquainted with that area too," he said.

It seemed he'd hunted and fished that part of the country. We sat down and talked some more, and I don't know whether I asked him if he was married or whether he asked me, but I do know that we were both curious.

When the question came up I said, "I'm married and I'm separated from my husband."

"How long?" he asked.

"Since last May," I said.

He had been separated from his wife since the previous May too, so as the followers of Yogi say—or is it Yoga?—we must have been vibrating on the same plane. I've found out since that Six liked me the first time he met me too. "I thought maybe, you being an actress, you'd start talking about yourself and never get off the subject," he said. "You didn't do that."

When we left the party along toward morning, Six's date had somehow gotten mixed up with some other group, and Holden, Six, and I left together. Doc wanted to go home, so we dropped him off at his apartment. After that I was taken hungry. I'd been so excited at the party I hadn't eaten so Six took me to the open-all-night Hamburg Heaven on Fifty-sixth Street. We sat at the counter and ate hamburgers and yakked. He told me about Continental Airlines, of which he's president, and his other business enterprises. In addition to Continental Airlines, he's in the oil business; he's chairman of the board of Swan-Finch Oil Corporation. He is also an independent oil producer. When we came out, the sun was up and people were going to early Mass. We'd sat there for a couple or three hours.

A week later, before flying back to Denver by way of Washington, he had lunch with me at my apartment. Then when he got to Washington he called me long distance, and when he reached Denver he phoned me from there. After that we saw each other every time he came into New York. It was nothing steady, for in the meantime I was going out with other people. But little by little I began to think, *Something serious is going to come of this.*

Then, in 1952, I took a trip to Mexico and got my divorce. Six got his divorce in Colorado a month before mine was filed. His divorce became final in September of 1952. We were married in March 1953.

That's the story of how I met Mr. Six. I'd do it over again tomorrow, even though it meant moving away from New York. A lot of people peg me wrong. They have the impression that I don't need anybody. This is not true. I'm just like every other human being: if you accomplish something you want somebody to share it with.

After all, living in Cherry Hills, just outside of Denver, is not like living in the country. It's only a few minutes from town. If it's winter in New York, you can put on a mink coat and the cold still penetrates, but in Denver it can be nine below and, if you're dressed for it, it's clear and wonderful and you feel warm. I love it there. It makes my spirits fizz.

About the only things I miss in Denver are the entertainment they have back East, for we don't have a Morocco, or a Stork Club, or a 21 in the Mile-High City. But we do have the Emerald Room in the Brown Palace Hotel where they have outstanding big-time entertainment, particularly in winter. Last winter they had Kay Thompson, the Wiere Brothers, Evelyn Knight, and

Mary McCarty. Aside from that, almost all Denver entertaining is done in the home. When Six opened our house with a house-warming, we invited 145 people.

And I do miss my mom and pop. They miss me too. My dad is this kind of man: he never tells me how much he misses me, but I know he does. I talk to him on the phone a lot, but that's not the same thing as seeing him.

Our Denver home was built in 1927, in a sort of Normandy architecture. When we bought it and moved in, we didn't have to do any remodeling. It's put together like the Rock of Gibraltar, only more comfortable. It's got a lot of hand-carved oak inside, and it's set in six acres of landscaped ground. This figure fits my husband's name, which is why my daughter Ethel came up with the idea of calling it Six Acres. It was a kind of a beige color inside before, so we did a complete interior paint job. Now it's all gayed up with chintzes, the walls are turquoise, and, to me, it's mighty pretty.

If you could overhear the pet names I call Bob Six in private, you'd think I'm crazy. So what? I think a husband and wife ought to be crazy—about each other. He does everything for me. Last summer, when I thought my appendix was about to bust, he took care of me like a male nurse. And he takes an interest in my work. He doesn't expect anything out of it; he's just interested in me and in what happens to me. I don't want to sound too girlish about it, but I simply adore the guy.

And I'm interested in his business, too, and in his successes. Recently he was appointed director of a bank and of an oil company. I was as proud as if I had achieved a personal triumph of my own. When I met him I used to pray that someday we'd get together. I'm happy it worked out that way.

He thrives on excitement. He's here one day, in New York the next, and three days later he's in Los Angeles. Two days after that he's back in Denver. He'd miss it if he didn't have to do it.

He has other sides too. He's a wonder with a barbecue spit. I can plan a good meal, but in a kitchen, with the sauces and the soup stock—no! I can cook eggs, but not a whole meal. However, nobody misses my cheffing, because Six can cook anything. He's outstanding—even in a part of the country where little boys learn to simmer barbecue sauce before they learn to draw a bead on the little boy next door with a cap pistol. One night last summer at Walter Lang's house in Beverly Hills, Six broiled steaks for eighteen people, among them such steak connoisseurs as Clark Gable and Tyrone Power. Next day Fieldsie Lang, Walter Lang's wife, called up to thank him. "I've been getting calls from my guests all morning," she said. "And they all said they've never tasted such steaks."

He can't tell you how he makes his barbecue sauce—I don't think he ever makes it the same way twice—but however he does it, it's out of this world. He has a closet in the kitchen in which he keeps all his little seasonings lined up. That's his closet, and woe to anyone who messes around in it. And Six does corn on the cob and a mixed green salad that are so good it's a wonder somebody hasn't made them illegal.

If I've low-rated myself as a cook, I'm willing to take a bow as a housewife. In my time, I've done most of the unpleasant things around a home that women like to shirk. I don't mean seeing to it that the laundry goes out and comes back, and that the supper is on the table and the husband gets it smoking hot when he wants it. These things I'm good at, but I've also gotten down on my hands and knees and scrubbed the floor when the help has quit unexpectedly.

But while I leave the steaks to Six, I have my own ideas of how to give a party. I like to stir different types of people into any group I invite. If all of my guests are movie executives or movie actors, the men will get together in a corner and talk movies and leave the women talking to each other. This is an abnormal situation and not my idea of a party at all. But if you've got a group where some talk show business, some talk politics, some talk investments, and some talk horse racing, or whatever, it keeps people milling around and that's good.

I know hostesses who think they're begging for trouble if they invite what they call "a mixed group." This leads up to what's the definition of a mixed group. After all, how can you get a more mixed group than by asking both men and women? I guess what the average person means by "a mixed group" is one in which most of the people don't know each other. That's all unnecessary fear. I ask show people and writers and brokers or lawyers or rainmakers or publicity workers to my parties; whoever happens to be my friends. They don't have to have anything in common but knowing me and a mutual dislike for phonies.

To get down to party-tossing brass tacks. I don't believe in having too many chairs. If some of your guests have to join each other on the floor, it makes for a more intimate party. The less chichi the better, I say. It's also a good idea to clear the decks for

227

action by shoving the furniture and knickknacks to one side, so you've got open floor space. This is particularly necessary for a cocktail party. For some unknown reason, people like to huddle in the middle of the floor at a martini-and-manhattan fight—that is, those who are not lined up in a solid wall of humanity at the bar.

Another must when I give a party at my home is big ash trays. I like to have them as big as dinner plates.

If I fling a party on an afternoon, and the guests are invited from five-thirty to seven-thirty, and if at midnight there're still twenty or more guests clinging to the ship, it's been a good party. If they linger on and don't want to go home, it proves they're comfortable and not bored. A hostess who says, " 'By now," and makes the late stayers punch the time clock and go home is silly. Mine can stick around as long as they want. It's all right by me.

Nor am I the kind of hostess who rushes from guest to guest organizing things, introducing people, and planning games. I'm not the busy-as-a-bird-dog-type hostess whose hostess pains come every five minutes. But I do like to make sure that people have a drink and that they're not sitting off in a corner by themselves, wishing they'd stayed home with the TV set.

If it's a big party, I usually hire a small orchestra, or if it's a cocktail party, I have a piano player in or an accordion player. I never ask anyone to sing. If anybody wants to get up and sound off, that's their business. I want no one to have the impression that he or she has been invited to a party of mine to perform. I've gotten too much of that routine myself. I've been to a lot of places where I know I was only asked with the expectation that I'd bring my pianist. Usually I went along with the gag, but I don't commit the same sin myself.

Now about those lil' old canapés, the ones that get soggy before the crowd can snap them up. One of the advantages of having caterers in for a blowout is that they keep making these dinguses fresh all the time and, speaking of soggy, it's nice to have a sprinkling of congenital hams on your guest list, to keep things crisp. Such go-go-go people keep a party alive, and if things threaten to dull up you can count on them to do their stuff. My favorite ham is the comedian Jack Pearl. He's wonderful at a party. Once he starts telling stories he never stops. Billy Gaxton and Danny Kaye are sensational, too, and Frank Sinatra is a big help. Just before I left California last August, Clifton Webb threw a party, and Frankie stood beside the piano with his cigarette and his highball, and entertained for an hour. Among the helpful hams at any party are Judy Garland, and there's always me. Judy will sing all night, and so will I.

Fortunately my children, Bobby and Ethel, didn't mind moving to Denver. Little Ethel is different from me. She's an outdoor girl at heart. She loves to get out to the country or go to the beach, any place as long as it's away from traffic.

The custody of the children is divided this way: I have them with me during the school year, and Levitt has them during the summer vacation if he so wishes. Last summer, when I had to go to Hollywood to work in the film *There's No Business Like Show Business*, I planned to take the children with me, although Denver is such a beautiful place in summer with its clear non-sticky, non-humid air that it seemed a shame to drag Bobby and Little

Ethel away from it. Still, if I left them in Denver all summer, I wouldn't be with them, and their stepfather would be spending long weekends with me in Beverly Hills and traveling east to Washington and New York and elsewhere on business. And this meant that there were times when nobody would be with them— nobody related to them, I mean.

So Levitt did a very nice thing. When he found that I'd be stuck in Hollywood, he leased a house in Rye, New York, so the children could have a pleasant summer place in which to stay. He didn't say he'd done it for that reason, but I know what it must have meant to him in the way of unselfishness and self-sacrifice because he's so dead set against commuting. To Levitt, a person doesn't have to go very far from Times Square to start battling the wilderness. Once when we were thinking about moving from 25 Central Park West to another apartment, he refused to move any farther up than Seventieth Street, and when Seventy-fifth Street was suggested to him he said, "I'm not going to live *that* far up." So leasing a house as far north as Rye was like renting a sod cottage on the tundra to him; it was quite a gesture.

Now that she's approaching her early teens, Little Ethel insists upon being called just Ethel without the "Little." They get that way about twelve or thirteen—dignity is the order of the day. No more pet names, see! But Little Bobby is still a rapscallion; dignity and hooey are one and the same thing to him.

One day early last summer at nine o'clock in the morning, I put Little Bobby and Little Ethel on a non-stop plane bound from Los Angeles to New York. They were scheduled to arrive in New York at seven-fifteen that night. Their father was to meet them at Idlewild Airport and drive them to Rye. I figured I'd give them two hours to get there. I waited; then, like the clucking mother hen that I am, I put in a person-to-person call to Little Ethel at six-fifteen California time. That was nine-fifteen New York time.

Someone answered the phone—it must have been the maid—and told the operator that Little Ethel was expected at nine o'clock but that she wasn't there yet. I left a number for her to call and waited until eight o'clock Pacific Coast time. I had to go out to dinner then, but I left the number of the house where I was going to be with the operator in the Beverly Hills Hotel. Every half hour I was called to the phone to hear the operator say, "Sorry, we haven't been able to complete your call. Your party has not arrived."

I went through torture, and tried not to think what might be going on.

People asked me afterward, "Why didn't you call the air line and find out where they were?" The trouble is, when you do that, you get the air line's "operations" department, and somebody says, "Sorry, the flight hasn't been completed, modom."

You already know *that*. Why else would you call, for chr-ying out loud? But they give you no details, and that makes the strain even worse. I tried to console myself with the thought that maybe Levitt had taken the kids to 21 for dinner or somewhere before taking them to Rye. Thank God I had that in mind, otherwise I'd have gone nuts; for Little Bobby's wisecracking, just before they took off, was still chewing at the back of my thoughts.

When I'd put them on the plane at the Los Angeles International Airport, Little Bobby, who's quite a tease, said, "Just think, only seven hours and fifteen minutes non-stop to New York." He'd looked at Little Ethel and said scornfully, "And you'll be throwing up all the way—that is, if we don't crash!" Poor Little Ethel. She doesn't get airsick all the time, but she can do without airplanes. I've seen her on flights when she was fine, but at other times she certainly gets airsick.

Many times that night I thought of Bobby's "if we don't crash." Finally, at ten-thirty Pacific Coast time—one-thirty New York time—my call went through.

"What happened?" I asked the children.

"An engine conked out," Ethel said. "And we were forced down in Cincinnati for a two-hour stopover. They couldn't repair the plane there, so they switched us to a two-motor job from Cincinnati to New York."

Then Mother's little comforter, Bobby, got on the phone and said, "Oh boy, Mom! Big deal! We flew in an airplane with only two motors."

When I went out to Hollywood to work in *No Business Like Show Business*, Six let me have the car he uses for mountain driving around Colorado and Wyoming. Before each rear wheel there's a piece of tubing which connects with two five-gallon cans of sand in the trunk. There's a lever on the dashboard which pulls out for mountain driving on slippery roads. And if you pull this lever sand comes through the rubber tubes in front of your rear wheels so you won't skid. There's no way of shutting that sand off once you've given it the word "Go." Of course I never had to use it in Beverly Hills but Dan Dailey was so fascinated with what would happen if I *did* that he circulated the story that I *had*. Dan's story goes that, after trying it once, I put the car back in the garage and said the hell with it. But while this never happened, Dan did have some fun with Bob's car. Dan and Donald O'Connor and Johnnie Ray and a few other conspirators pulled a trick on me. We'd been working down at Western Avenue and when we were dismissed at six o'clock at night the whole crew came out to watch me drive away. I wondered, "What are they looking at?" but I couldn't think of an answer.

I'm out on Sunset Boulevard, near the Beverly Hills Hotel, and I'm driving along in this twelve-cylinder hot rod when all of a sudden I hear birds singing. I came to a stop light, stopped the car, and the birds piped down. Then I put my foot on the gas and there was more twittering and bird calls, and people looking at me as if I'm an idiot.

When I pulled up in front of the hotel, I said to Bruce, one of the outside boys, "There's something wrong with this car. It's like canaries singing. If you find out what it is, let me know."

What those clowns had done was this: they'd put a bird whistle in each exhaust. There were two on the car, but when I started the motor one of them had fallen out. The other one didn't go into action until I hit Sunset Boulevard, so the joke was on the jokesters, since nothing happened while they were looking and listening.

But movie making is not all high jinks, skylarking, and elaborate impractical jokes. It can be rugged while it's going on. You don't have to go through a movie six times a week (or eight

233

with matinees) but the thing about a movie is that while you're working in it it's concentrated and it packs a lot of effort into a short time. For example, take one day's shooting for the finale of *There's No Business Like Show Business.* For that finale I wore a dress that weighed fifteen pounds.

The camera picked us up coming down a flight of enormously wide and high stairs, but in order to get to the top of those steps in the first place and start coming down, we first had to climb a ladder hidden out of camera view. That is, it was a cross between a ladder and a stairway. The steps didn't rise on a gradual incline, they were almost on top of each other. We had to start climbing with the second step from the bottom so we'd have the right action as we came over the top in range of the camera. Don't ask me why, except that it was part of getting in gear with the starting of the tempo of the words "Standing out in front on opening nights." And the way we were doing it, "Show Biz" was strictly a rhythm song. My wardrobe girl, Josephine, had to hold my dress up in back to keep me from stepping on it and I had to hold it up in front. Four or five steps from the top Josephine let go. After that I was on my own. Marching up those almost perpendicular steps was *something*.

When we got to the point where we started down the steps, we had to come down without looking as we sang, ". . . even with a turkey that you know will fold." We couldn't bend our knees. We had to hold ourselves poker straight. Finally we got that too.

I suppose we went up and down thirty times. Not only did my dress weigh fifteen or twenty pounds, like I said, I had to protect

234

it too. If I'd stepped on it, I would have stepped on thousands of bucks.

And while I'm on the subject of filming *There's No Business Like Show Business*, there's The Case of Marilyn Monroe and the "Right Choreographer." Fox had difficulty in getting a choreographer for her who made her happy. They had Bob Alton handling the choreography for everyone else in the picture but Marilyn shook her pretty head. She'd had luck before with Jack Cole, who goes in for a kind of Javanese or Balinese peckin' with the head. It's hard to blueprint it; all I know is that every time I try it I get a crick in the neck.

As Dan Dailey put it: "So she decided she wanted Cole instead of Bob Alton, because she wanted everything going, and she didn't think Alton gave her a chance to keep everything going." This summing up of the situation conjured up a picture of all parts of her body moving at the same time. This picture came pretty close to matching the facts in the "Heat Wave" number she did in the film.

Alton had had her whole number laid out. His assistant had demonstrated it to the producer and to the director, and they'd flipped, they thought it so great. Alton had not one, not two, but four guys slappin' the tom-toms for Marilyn, but she didn't like it. She didn't put it quite the way Dan Dailey put it; but she said she "wanted more movement in it." And she wanted Jack Cole to do the choreography for the number. She'd done all right with Jack in the "Diamonds Are a Girl's Best Friend" number in *Gentlemen Prefer Blondes* and, having done all right with him once, she figured she'd be safer with him again. She got him.

235

Storywise, Alton didn't want her dancing to be *that* broad. She was playing a girl who'd fallen in love with our son, Donald O'Connor (Dan Dailey and I were Donald's parents) in the picture. In the story I was against this girl because she had stolen our number; we were supposed to do "Heat Wave," but she'd ended with it. Also storywise, if her dancing got a little too sexy with the bumps and grinds the audience would think (and it would be natural for Dan and me as Donald's parents to think it too), *This is not the girl for our boy.* After all, Dan and Donald and I were supposed to be a real, down-to-earth, good American vaudeville family, so for the picture's sake Alton didn't want her dance to be too sultry. But Marilyn wanted it the other way, and at that point the studio was doing its goldarnedest to keep her happy.

Oh well.

No matter how heavy my dresses were, or how many ladders I had to climb in them, there was little emotional stress and strain involved in working in a Walter Lang picture. The emphasis is not on the heavies. They're happy pictures. You're surrounded by people you like. No one hears Lang raise his voice nor do you hear him tell an actor how to do a scene. He gets his results by going over and exchanging a few soft words with the men or women in his cast. I don't know how the person to whom he's talking hears him because he's so quiet, but they get what he means.

Chapter Seventeen

Earlier in this story I said that when I was asked to be the vocal soloist in the First George Gershwin Memorial Concert it was one of the high points of my life. Another peak as high was the night in 1953 when I appeared on a two-hour Ford Company television show with Mary Martin. It turned out to be the first "spectacular" TV show, although they didn't call it that then. That show made TV history in a number of ways, but before I tell about it I want to talk about me and radio briefly. I notice that I've said almost nothing about it until now.

A lot of people wondered why radio didn't snap me up quicker and keep me busier than it did. "Was it because you could only go on Sunday nights or week nights after the last curtain of your show," they ask, "and this meant being rushed across town to a broadcasting station behind a police escort with screaming sirens?"

The truth is that there was an idea going around that my voice was too brassy for radio; that I came through with such a vocal belt that I'd knock out the sending apparatus. Like, for instance, I'd planned to sing "Blow, Gabriel, Blow," which is a number with high notes, as part of a guest shot, but when I got to the broadcasting studio and was ready to do it they made me lower my key. They told me that if I did it the way I did it on the stage it would blow the fuses.

In other words, the news was passed that I was too loud and too brazen for radio. Crooners and gals with soft voices were the thing. Years went by—in fact, television was with us—before they said, "Look, if you're going to go on the air, you should sing the way you've always sung on the stage. If you tone your voice down, the public will ask, 'What happened to this dame with the big voice we've heard so much about?' "

Finally they found out that if they didn't take me the way I am they weren't going to get much of anything. It was only by taking a firm grip on myself that I kept from saying, "Now you're telling me! By what stroke of genius have you finally arrived at the conclusion that I can only be myself if nobody turns my damper down?" And I didn't take a firm grip on myself.

I had the same trouble with my earlier movies, remember? I've gone into what Hollywood did to me and what I didn't do to Hollywood, but the way it sounds best to me is the way one guy put it: "For some reason, Miss Merman has never been able to do full justice to herself in the movies. Perhaps the fact that she has been so far away from New York has depressed her, just as it depressed the New Yorkers. More probably it's because no camera has yet been invented large enough to capture her spirits."

But to get back to radio. Even if radio had wanted me, even if I'd been in as brisk demand as Charlie McCarthy, I wasn't one of those grasshopper actresses always willing to drop everything—even if it meant walking out on a Broadway show—to go on radio, to make records, or to dash out to Hollywood. When I had a job I stayed with it. I took almost no vacations.

In the days to come I may score some successes in TV and I may lose a couple of decisions to that medium, but come what may, some of the reviewers said that the two-girl show I did with Mary Martin was the greatest thing ever heard on TV up to that time. And they can't take that back. One TV critic said, "It was a fabulously happy combination of talent and inspiration." The sponsor, the Ford Motor Company, bought out the two big networks for the occasion. All the shows on those two chains were canceled and sixty million people listened and looked.

There was Mary with her sweet-type voice and her special type rhythm, and me with my lusty pipes, and believe it or not we blended. Leland Hayward put the show together as deftly and as skillfully as a chef assembles a soufflé—if that's what a chef does to a soufflé. Jerome Robbins did the choreography; the orchestra conductor, Jay Blackton, helped Mary and me get our duet effects; and Decca made a recording of it as we did it, taking it right off the air.

The applause on the Decca disk comes through exactly the way the public heard our live audience do it that night. To me, that crowd reaction was spine-fingering and I loved those countermelodies, where Mary sang one thing and I sang another simultaneously, and yet we made music together. Mary did it to "Tea for Two" while I did it to "You're Not Sick, You're Just in Love"; and we interlaced "Stormy Weather" with "Indian Love Call."

We rehearsed for two weeks, but we didn't concentrate altogether on our melodic sequence because Mary and I did other things in the show; the record of our singing together represented only the closing of a two-hour period. The recording was my idea. I called up Si Rady, a Decca executive, and said, "Listen, Mary and I've got quite a thing here. I wish you'd come to the rehearsal and see if you don't think it worth pressing." So he came down, heard the rehearsal, and enthused.

After the performance at New York's Center Theater, the sponsor, Henry Ford II, threw a party at the Waldorf-Astoria. It was a thoughtful gesture. Mr. Ford took over the whole Wedgewood Room, as well as the other room that opens off a balcony as you enter through the front lobby. There were tables loaded with masses of white flowers, and there was Lester Lanin and a thirty-piece orchestra. Everything was done in a very large way.

But in the midst of all this grandeur a funny incident happened. Two hours before we went on the air, Mary Martin's husband, Dick Halliday, staggered into my dressing room lugging a huge thing of flowers. I'd never seen anything like it. It was so big I couldn't even see the basket that held it. It could have been a floral shroud for a horse. Halliday brought this portable garden in, and said, "You may have this for fifteen minutes!"

"How do you mean, fifteen minutes?" I asked.

He showed me the card attached to it, and it was clear that

somebody had booted one: whether one of Mr. Ford's secretaries or not, I don't know. I imagine Mr. Ford had told someone to send out four of those floral monsters: one to Marian Anderson, another to Dorothy Stickney, another to Mary Martin, and still another to me, since we were all featured in the festivities. But all it said on the card was: "Good luck and best wishes tonight to: Mary Martin, Ethel Merman, Marian Anderson, and Dorothy Stickney. From Henry Ford II." So it was obvious that someone had plumbered, and as a result one large economy-size floral piece was being delivered to the four of us.

"After you've had this for fifteen minutes," Halliday said, "I'll send it to Dorothy Stickney and let her have it for fifteen minutes. After that, Marian Anderson can have it for fifteen minutes."

In the end, it wound up at my place. Dick and Mary Martin were driving up to Connecticut after the show; they didn't have a florist's truck, and with all the other flowers Mary received, there wasn't room in their car for Mr. Ford's all-purpose economy-size floral tribute. Mary said to me, "You take it," so I took it.

Afterward people who saw and heard Mary and me sing our songs together told me that the simplicity of the thing was what got them. I was on stage right and Mary was on stage left; behind me was a big poster of *Call Me Madam*. On her side was a poster from *South Pacific*. The camera picked me up at the opening and I sang "There's No Business Like Show Business," Mary sang "I'm in Love with a Wonderful Guy," and we walked downstage together to where there were two stools like bar stools. I perched on one and Mary sat on the other, and we sang thirty-three of the greatest popular songs ever written.

241

It did things to people. Some of the viewers told me afterward that they cried.

There were those who seemed to think it an impressive feat that Mary and I rendered all of those songs from memory. Sometimes, in television, you have cue cards to jog you if you blank out. Mary and I didn't need them. Those words had been pounded into our brains to stay.

After such a show it was tough for me that in my 1954 TV debut I was handled as if I were competing with the Jo Staffords, the Dinah Shores, and the Joni Jameses of this world. I was treated like a popular recording artist who sings popular songs to a hysterically enthusiastic audience after they've been selected by a recording company's pop division.

Some of these pop-singer personalities have never been in a stage show (even summer stock) or in the movies and they have no sense of dramatic value, yet in their own field they're tops. We're living in a specialized world, and I can understand why each person who can be a specialist is one. I have my own specialty and it isn't pop records, even though I was being handled as such. They were having me do vaudeville sketches, instead of the thing I'd done in nine straight New York hit stage shows.

Yes, sir, they had me doing the kind of sketches you see on a Milton Berle show, on a Jack Benny show, or on a Jackie Gleason show. Me, a dame who has always played a character in a story. Maybe sometimes the story was skimpy and screwy but nevertheless that's what my songs had grown out of. So what happened? So, not playing a character, I had no emotional effect on TV audiences. I'd sing a big song like "I Got Rhythm" and it meant

242

nothing to the audience because they didn't know what I was talking about. The other artists, the Sinatras, the Perry Comos, the Frankie Laines, the Jo Staffords, and the Dinah Shores came out and sang the latest hit-record song, and they were home. They didn't have to be in love with anyone in a story to lend their song impact or meaning, but my songs are best when the audience is cued into them.

When I sing merely a love song or rhythm song with no motivation or build-up I have nothing extra going for me. To make people like the thoughts in the song I sing, I have to play a character they like first, in a play.

When I wanted a fellow, as I did in *Annie*, I won that fellow after a struggle. I was the girl who fell in love. When I sang "They Say That Falling in Love Is Wonderful" and my beau sang "The Girl That I Marry" to me, that meant that I was the girl the audience was pulling for. In nine hit Broadway musicals I had channeled my personality through a story line, not through a revue of strung-together sketches, but in spite of this, in my first TV appearance after my debut with Mary Martin, the thing that had made me successful on Broadway was junked and I found myself trying to cash in on the thing that made the other babes successful.

Apparently it was hard for those who hired me to think of me as Ethel Merman. They seemed to have me mixed with Imogene Coca. I found myself singing "I Got Rhythm" as a lead into a sight gag. Every time I opened my mouth and held a note for sixteen bars, vases broke and pictures fell from the walls.

After that miserable experience, a pal of mine, a great song

243

writer and producer, Jule Styne, decided this type of thing was wrong for me, and Leland Hayward, who was one of the program executives for NBC, arranged for me to do *Anything Goes* on TV. There was a very good cast, with Frank Sinatra playing my boy friend as a sort of *Pal Joey* character. But, having signed Sinatra, they discovered that there weren't any songs in the score for him because Sinatra had the part Billy Gaxton had on the stage and Gaxton hadn't really sung in the original play although he had cooed a song, a dilly called "All through the Night," with Bettina Hall. They changed that and condensed it into an hour; three extra songs were interpolated from other Cole Porter shows, and when we got through it all hung together in one piece. They hired Bert Lahr to take the Victor Moore part and they interpolated a song for Bert too. It all made sense and it got good reviews. I was a definite character in it with a definite personality.

I was very happy with Jule in that production, and I gather that he was happy with me, for it was Jule who once said of me, "I feel she's a female George M. Cohan." You can't ask for much better than that, can you?

I've discovered that you have to give yourself completely to TV because it takes so much out of you. Television is a brain picker, and you have to like what you're doing in it to do it right. The success of any television program is based on enthusiasm. Many other things are based on enthusiasm too but in other things, such as a movie studio, you have many people working for every one in television. The TV production staff is much smaller; and TV production boys have to do a lot of their own chores, whereas in a movie studio they have all kinds of outside help.

244

In addition to Jule Styne, I can always count on a helping hand from a pro named Roger Edens when I'm up against a TV problem or a concert date. If you've stayed with me from the start, you'll remember that it was Roger who played piano for me in my first stage success, *Girl Crazy*. After Al Siegel got sick Roger also made arrangements and played for me at the Central Park Casino, in the days when Jimmy Walker was New York's mayor. Roger is a Mr. Big at M-G-M now, a top-flight producer of musicals, no less, but he's never too busy to help me. Occasionally I pick up a phone and tell him, "I'm on radio next week," or "I'm on a TV show. How's about fixing me up something I can use?" I did the whole thing of "I Love Paris" in a TV show with an Edens arrangement.

If Roger can spare the time, he kicks through. He's up to his neck as an M-G-M producer, but it doesn't take a lot of time for him to help me because he knows me and my needs so well. When I was still in New York and Roger had gone to Hollywood, I'd call him long distance and tell him, "I'm going to open at the Strand," or "I'm going to open at the Paramount, and I need an arrangement," and Roger would pick up a song with a fast tempo or a click ballad and think up a great arrangement. Then he'd drop into one of those disk mills where they cut a record of your voice, or of you playing an instrument, and he played the piano and sang, bless his heart. And he'd wind up with a recording of the way he thought my performance ought to sound complete with suggested tempo. Then he'd make a lead sheet of it and airmail the whole thing to me. For those who don't know what a lead sheet is, it's the melody written out. I'd give his record to an arranger and when I got the arrangement back I'd play it and Roger's record over and I'd cock an ear at his retards and his changes in tempo, until I'd learned the whole ball of wax.

So far as I know, nobody else does it this way, and it's still amazing to me that it can be done. Only a year or two ago Roger worked his remote-control-stuff stunt for me for a show I did in Dallas, Texas. He whipped up an opening called "Lady with a Song."

He had already written a musical introduction for me with lyrics to use when I'd worked a concert at Denver's Red Rocks, which is Denver's equivalent of the Hollywood Bowl. When I S.O.S.'d Roger about my Texas date, he took that Red Rocks material and rewrote it, gearing it to Dallas. When he was through with it, it was called *You're in Texas*, and he'd changed the lyrics of "Lady with a Song" to make them more appropriate. Then he recorded the results and sent them to me in Denver. I played it all and learned it. That night I called him long distance. I asked him, "Want to hear something?" and sang it to him.

I could hear him going "boinng" over the phone. "It's impossible that you've learned it so quickly!" he said.

"O.K.," I said. "So it's impossible. I'm a quick study."

Of course you can't do such things unless you get hold of someone who knows exactly what you want and what you can do and what's good for you—all of which Roger knows about me. He's always been a man with a big talent, but he's just come into his own as the producer of Metro's film featuring Helen Traubel, José Ferrer, and Merle Oberon. It is called *Deep in My Heart* and it's been a big money-maker.

Having a talent like Roger behind you is a wonderful thing, but it's not the answer to the ambitious girls who write me to ask for what they call "the secret of your success." I don't have any advice for girls who want to be successful sopranos or contraltos. I'm not selfish about this. You can't explain your personality any more than you can give away pieces of your larynx. If I were going to advise such kids, I'd suggest that they get a George Gershwin, a Cole Porter, or an Irving Berlin to write their songs for them. If I told them anything else, it would probably be the wrong thing and I'd be blamed for it.

Cole Porter says that when I'm singing my face "takes on a transfixed look," as if I'm in heaven. "A whole different, new kind of soft-inside Merman shines through when she sings," he says. I'll go this far in agreeing with him: I feel wonderful when I use my pipes, the way Bing Crosby feels when he plays golf or the way I imagine Babe Ruth felt when he was taking his cut at the ball. When a song comes out of me, I enjoy it. I don't think there's anything wrong in that.

I stuck as close as glue to Gershwin, Berlin, and Porter. I like to think that part of their success has been due to me. Certainly part of my success was due to them. I've always tried to operate with successful people. I see nothing sinful in trying to pick associates that are right for you and who can help you achieve your goal.

I will say this much: "Try to get with a good agent. See if you can get an audition. If you sing good when the right people listen, and they think you have possibilities, they'll do something about it. If they think you have no possibilities, they'll be honest and tell you."

Another part of getting ahead is getting the breaks. Nobody can tell you how to do that. I got my first breaks in a place called the Little Russia, and in a show produced by Vinton Freedley, with songs by a man named Gershwin. There's no more Little Russia; Gershwin is dead; and Freedley is not as active as he once was.

The truth is, a phrase like "the secret of your success" is just a phrase; it doesn't mean any more than the saying "The show must go on." I don't want to give the idea that these five words are unimportant or that I take their meaning casually. I didn't miss a day in my last show and it ran for a couple of years. I went right through it, and if I had some of the usual problems that gals have, I ignored them. I just hitched up my pants and kept right on working.

But oceans of hooey have been spilled about living up to the "show-must-go-on" slogan. To me, it's an overplayed cliché. The thing that counts is to keep in there pitching, whether you're on a stage or not. Show business is no more important than any other business. In other businesses there's no question about "going on." The work goes on in spite of toothache, heartbreak, and losing loved ones. There's no point of singling out show biz and making a big dramatic thing of it.

When I worked for Caleb Bragg at the B. K. Vacuum Booster Brake Company on Long Island, I went to work unless I was too sick to stand up. So did Mr. Bragg. So did everybody else who worked there. It wasn't supposed to be noble. It was what average people did. They'd have been ashamed to do anything else.

My job happens to be show biz, but it's the same deal. I go on and stay on until my part is finished. I may not feel well, but it doesn't occur to me not to go for a wardrobe fitting unless a doctor tells me I can't. What's so remarkable about that? It's my job, isn't it? I've got a contract to fulfill, haven't I? I knew what I was doing when I signed the contract, and I'm getting paid for it.

Anyone's life is full of stuff that can lay him or her low. Anyone can wake up telling himself, *I'm worried*, or *I feel awful*, but he keeps on working anyhow. When my little daughter Ethel had the hives so bad that she was in great pain, I was out there on the stage putting it out. I found myself crying, thinking about that little stinker tossing and turning back home, but I kept on making people laugh anyhow.

Every time I try to persuade my father to quit work and take it easy, I run into a sample of the instinct everyone has to keep on doing his job. When I ask him, "Why don't you and Mom move out West and live with me?" he says, "I can't. Don't you realize I have a job, Ethel?"

"Please stop talking about that job," I say. "You don't have to have that job."

"What would I do just sitting around home?" he asks. "I'd fold, Ethel. My job keeps me alive."

I can see his point. He's with his cronies every day, and his work isn't laborious. He only uses his head figuring, so it doesn't

249

use him up physically and it keeps his mind occupied. Besides, it's his obligation. Do you think he'd leave that? So when I say to him, "Why don't you and Mom hop on an airplane and visit me for a couple of weeks?" he answers, "It's inventory time, Ethel," or "I've got to get a statement out." See?

Come hell or high water, his show is going on right to the end.

Sometimes it takes guts—if you'll pardon the expression—to keep putting out when everything seems to be against you, but if you stay with it the satisfaction you get pays you for what it's taken out of you. Which reminds me of a thing that happened in Washington, D.C., during the four-week run of *Call Me Madam* there. At a luncheon given by a group of press women, one of the dames asked me "What's the secret of your distinctive singing style?" I told her I didn't know. I said that I'd been singing that way since I was five and all I knew was that my voice seemed to get stronger instead of weaker.

Then another of those press dolls asked me to give them a sample of "the voice you've been using since you were five," and I said, "I'm sorry, but I have no accompaniment." That didn't stop them.

Somebody else said, "How's about singing 'Show Business' without an accompaniment?"

Now "Show Business" is hard to do without accompaniment. You talk half of it instead of singing it, so it's easy to get off key. It's even harder to get back on key again, with no music to pull you back on. I was scared stiff, but I was on a spot. I could have said, "I didn't catch the name. Is it Mrs. Legree?" or something discouraging. But I didn't want to be one of those singers who says, "Sorry, I didn't bring my music," when somebody requests a number, so I said, "O.K., I'll give it a tussle."

A male Washington reporter, a Mr. Ernie Schier, who happened to be present, wrote up what happened then for the Washington, D.C., *Times-Herald*. It went this way:

"Ethel read a short, good-humored speech, thanked the ladies for the honor they did her, and then the customary question and answer period began. Around about the fourth question some anonymous genius—who henceforth in my memory will rank with the great strategists of all time—thought to ask if the lady would give her listeners a sample of the voice she had described as 'the one I've been using since I was five years old.'

"A scattering of applause greeted the question but no one seemed to realize that the request was unreasonable without some form of accompaniment, and not one of Petrillo's boys was there. Ethel, smiling, started to back away, shaking her head. Then she started forward again, still smiling; okay, she seemed to say, why not? She stood with her hands resting on the podium for a minute, in her plain gray suit, looking no more prepossessing than any of the other ladies present. The vast room fell quiet. Ethel lifted up her head and opened her mouth. She started low and the words came out. 'There's no business like show business . . .' No piano, mind you, no music of any kind—just that magic voice. In a moment, the hesitance was gone. Sweet and clear, unencumbered by tricks, her voice soared across the room: 'Yesterday they told you you would not go far . . . that night you open and there you are . . . next day on your dressing room they've hung a star . . .' When she got to the end, 'Let's go on with the show!' you wondered why you hadn't been standing at attention while she was singing.

"They say greatness is an elusive quality, something impossible to describe. It wasn't yesterday when Ethel sang. You could see it, hear it, and feel it. To her, it was doing what came naturally. You knew then that she doesn't perform on the stage the way other actors do. The woman, the voice and the song were a part of each other.

"It was a song sung without coyness, without affectation. The innate honesty of the woman who was singing and the zest in her voice, if they could be captured in portrait, would serve as a classic of the meaning of a performer's life. It was a deeply stirring demonstration of what Ethel herself had described a few minutes earlier as the actor's urge to give, asking nothing for himself but what the audience chooses to return. As one of those present exclaimed, 'Who is this Kirsten Flagstad anyhow?' "

I'll settle for that.

Well, this seems as good a spot as any to ring down my curtain. I don't want anyone to have to twist my arm to get me off. I've said that when I'm done with a thing I write period after it. And so, brothers and sisters, period. I hope it's been nice knowing me.